INDIA'S CHANGING MEDIA LANDSCAPE

INDIA'S CHANGING MEDIA LANDSCAPE

Cross Media Ownership, FDI and Broadcast Bill

Dr. Ahsanul Haq Chishti

PARTRIDGE

ISBN: Hardcover   978-1-4828-8675-7
           Softcover   978-1-4828-8674-0
           eBook   978-1-4828-8673-3

To order additional copies of this book, contact
Partridge India
000 800 10062 62
orders.india@partridgepublishing.com

www.partridgepublishing.com/india

Foreword

Media ownership in India is extremely diverse. This is necessitated by the infinite diversity in cultures and languages across the sub-continent. Except for an occasional political party daily newspaper, the Indian print media is by and large owned by business families like the Birlas, the Jains, the Marans, the Sarkars and the Ramoji Raos.

Film production, distribution and exhibition too are largely family-owned. Public-owned electronic media ruled the roost until the early 1990s but since then the corporate media have been calling the shots. Prasar Bharati- run nationwide radio and television networks enjoy the widest reach but lack credibility, innovation, variety and sophistication.

During the last decade or so, however, consolidation and concentration as much as vertical and horizontal integration have marked the Indian media landscape. The pace has been set by the Ambani brothers, Bennett Coleman & Co Limited, the Jagran group, the Maran family, Viacom18, Star India and a host of significant but smaller players in the numerous languages and dialects of this diverse nation.

Why should this dominant trend towards concentration and integration through cross-media ownership be a concern for the quality and performance of the media? Because concentration in news outlets allows little or no diversity in content and plurality of perspectives which consequentially hampers the growth of aware citizenry and informed democracy.

Public policy research has few takers. While explicit policy is there for the public to see in published documents by various units of the Ministry of Information and Broadcasting, the more subtle implicit policy as seen in content and in execution of briefs and instructions from the powers that be, is rarely analysed.

Dr. Ahsanul Haq Chishti's book takes up the challenge of analysing public policy with regard to cross-media ownership in India. He makes out interesting case for the imperative need for some kind of regulation of cross-media ownership so as to ensure as much diversity in media as possible. Indeed, this has been the recommendation of the First and Second Press Commission Reports, the Chanda, Verghese and Joshi Reports and of the various drafts of Broadcasting bills under both Congress and BJP regimes. No government has, however, been bold enough to turn the bills into Acts. Parliament after parliament and regime after regime has made loud noises about reining in the trend of ownership concentration in media, but has not had the temerity to enforce regulation of cross-media ownership and diversity in content or even some kind of diversity in the newsroom.

In this book, Dr. Chishti comes up with, in his own unique flair of writing, an interesting story of the historical developments in Indian public policy on media ownership, making extensive use of published documents and reports and through surveys of, and interviews with, senior editors and journalists.

This publication is a welcome addition to the scant literature available on the subject and it would be particularly useful to policy planners, academicians, researchers equally and make an interesting read to the general readers as well.

KEVAL J. KUMAR
Professor Adjunct
Mudra Institute of Communication & Advertising, Ahmedabad
Formerly, Professor & Head, Symbiosis Institute of Journalism and Department of Communications & Journalism, Pune, India

To the everlasting memory of my illustrious father late **Noor ud Din Chishti**, who laid a strong edifice of values and principles in me that have ultimately shaped me and kindled an urge to seek more knowledge; whom I lost when I was too young to understand the loss of his separation!

And my mother **Hajra** in whose death I lost not only the vibrant youth and a cheerful face but also the cradle of life.

Acknowledgements

There are certain events in life for which a mere word of acknowledgement is not enough. My present book is one such example.

The subject being novel in nature in India with very few experts and practitioners having a command over it, getting them to share the same was not an easy task. But more than that was the magnanimity with which they dispensed with their busy schedules and shared their precious moments and experiences with me.

In this regard, Dr. Keval J. Kumar, Professor Adjunct, Mudra Institute of Communications, Ahmedabad and former head of Pune University's Communication & Journalism Department merits special mention. His support, advice and encouragement was something that mattered the most. Thanks to him for agreeing to write the foreword for the book despite his very busy schedule and prior commitments world over.

Media is an over stretched profession in which a practitioner always races against time. Thus in the end, as in the words of Dr. Viktor E. Frankl, author of bestseller *Men's Search for Meaning*, gets depersonalised. In such a situation I feel highly indebted to all those who spared the time and shared their experiences with me. I am grateful to late Dileep Padgaonkar, former editor, *The Times of India* and Chairman, Asia Pacific Communication Associates (APCA), New Delhi, for the valuable and thought provoking insight he provided on various aspects of Media industry in India and abroad. His views really opened new vistas of debate for me. May his soul rest in peace!

My sincere thanks also go to friends like Joseph Nathan, Editorial Advisor and Rimmi Bhasin, Corporate Secretary of the company for the help and information from time to time.

I am grateful to Ms. Payal Kohli, editor, *Cosmopolitan* for sharing her views on the subject. I would never forget how veteran journalist Swati Chaturvedi grappled with her busy schedule and provided important inputs on the subject.

My sincere thanks go to the officials of American Centre and British Council library, New Delhi who allowed me to use their references on the subject. I also take this opportunity to express my gratitude to the library staff of Indian Institute of Mass Communication, New Delhi, Central Secretariat Library, New Delhi and Mass Communication Research Centre, Jamia Millia Islamia, New Delhi for letting me avail their facilities. The research material and the co-operation provided by Mr. Saxena and his library at Press Institute of India were of immense help to me. Rather it laid the foundation of my research.

I am also grateful to Press Information Bureau, New Delhi and Srinagar and its officers for keeping me updated continuously on the official perspective of the subject.

My wife, Dr. Shahnaz Mufti, was keenly interested in my book and also enriched its draft with her own research experiences. She literally kept me on toes while I was preparing the final draft. I have no words to thank her.

I am extremely grateful to the management of Partridge Publishers, a division of Penguin International, for giving my thoughts a book form. My personal compliments go to Pohar Barua and Charm Revyi and for the patience they showed while working with me.

Dr. Ahsanul Haq Chishti
New Delhi, India

Contents

Preface

I ndian media is a booming industry. It is expanding like never before. If we go by statistics alone, the industry is expanding at a Compounded Annual Growth Rate of 13-14% presently and is poised to cross a volume of Rs. 2, 26, 000 crore by 2020. Already the industry size has doubled during the last five years. Among all the splits of the industry, the digital advertising grew by 38% during last year and is expected to perform well in coming years as well. Other sectors including print media are also expanding and doing well.

Ever since the first phase of economic liberalization in India, media industry in the country is growing exponentially. There are factors like opening of the industry to foreign investment which have excelled this growth. So far the Indian media industry has fetched a foreign investment of around Rs. 20, 000 crore and it is still coming.

But equally interesting is the fact that this whole phenomenon has been going on in the country without any laws governing it specifically. Even the Broadcast Bill which was framed way back in 1997 could not be tabled in the parliament till date despite it having been amended 19 times so far.

These are the interesting areas which I have tracked in this book. The history and evolution of the Broadcast Bill, how the government reversed its cabinet resolution of 1955 disallowing any foreign equity in Indian media and more importantly how this media growth has brought about an influencing change in the cultural sensibilities of the people and how the foreign channels brought with them a new style and fashion code.

The emergence of media in India as a business has led to the establishment of a variety of interpretations. Today journalists, academicians, activists and business writers alike write and interpret the media in India in publications, on-line discourses and websites, workshops and seminars. *Sage India* currently publishes a variety of books on communication—from empirical investigations to anthologies and other titles. Media news and stories are carried in a variety of business and trade magazines like *BusinessWorld, Business India* and financial papers like *The Economic Times* and *The Business Standard*, a range of current affairs magazines such as *India Today, Frontline* and *Outlook*, scholarly journals like *Economic and Political Weekly*, activist publications like *Voices* and *Madhyam* and other media outlets in English and other vernacular languages on regular basis.

Trade associations like FICCI and software companies like Tata Infosys along with a broad spectrum of websites like *www.thehoot.org, www.sarai.net*, etc. have been continuously publishing updates on media and news. This flurry of channels and space for media related stories is a comparatively recent phenomenon co- terminus with the Indian media industry's tryst with neo-liberalisation and privatization.

In India the Second Press Commission submitted its report to the Government in 1982. In its study the commission examined and studied about 245 reports and studies conducted on various aspects of Indian media. Of these just five pertained to the ownership question (Vol. II, Appendix. 1.35, p.p. 64). But some of these studies were either too localized to have a national impact or have lost relevance in the changed times.

But *Ownership & Control Structure of the Indian Press*, by S K Goyal & Chalapatti Rao (1981) of the Indian Institute of Public Administration, New Delhi gives an analytical account of the ownership pattern of the national press in India at that time.

Besides, trade body FICCI has been coming out with annual report on the status of Indian media and entertainment industry every year and this year's report(FICCI-KPMG-2016) has been duly incorporated in this book. Also the Telecom Regulatory Authority of India (TRAI) and Administrative Staff College of India (ASCI), Hyderabad have also dealt with the subject in their various reports which also have been referred to in this book. Similarly the

Open Society Foundation initiative (*Mapping Digital Media-Country Report-India-2013*) has been an incisive study on the emerging media scene in the country and its related issues.

This apart, the past decade and a half has seen massive changes on the media turf by way of changing ownership patterns, mergers, acquisitions, FDI and tie ups etc. These latest inputs are to be taken into account before making an opinion on the subject.

The changes or shift in the ownership pattern has had a cascading effect on the content and the human resource potential of the media industry, both having to adjust to the rules set by the new and emerging ownership patterns.

These issues have been explored in this book in a chapter wise scheme.

Chapter I deals with the theoretical definition of Cross Media Ownership, its types and applicability to the current scenario of media industry in India.

The chapter discusses, most importantly, the political consequences of media concentration by looking at cases like that of Rupert Murdoch and other such examples from countries like USA, Australia and England.

Chapter II gives a global perspective and sums up the worldwide situation on Cross Media Ownership. It profiles and analyses the pertinent laws of a number of countries related to Cross Media Ownership.

Chapter III tracks the history of ownership concentration in Indian media in the light of reports and studies by the First and Second Press Commissions, the Press Council of India (PCI) and the Registrar of Newspapers in India (RNI).

Chapter IV traces the evolution and stages of the Broadcast Bill and the legislative activities that led to its framing.

Chapter V sums up the current trends emerging in the Indian media industry which has been expanding since the opening up of the Indian economy two decades ago.

Chapter VI profiles some of the leading media barons of India. It gives a summarized account of the history, operations and market presence of some leading media brands in the country like Living Media India Ltd. of India Today and Aaj Tak fame, Reliance, Bennett Coleman & Co. Ltd., the owners of *The Times of India* and Times NOW, NDTV and ZEE.

Chapter VII gives out an empirical survey on the subject by the author. The survey throws up results stressing the need for diversity and plurality in media ownership. The survey also brings to focus the influence of ownership on the content output of a media outlet.

Chapter VIII wraps up the discussion with some broad conclusions, observations and recommendations for policy planners, decision makers and media analysts. Among these conclusions include the prevalence of Cross Media Ownership curbs in a number of countries in the world including some technologically advanced countries.

Ways of implementing the cross media restrictions through various equity caps and market share restrictions also form part of the recommendations. The need for a national level regulatory body to monitor the growing cross media tendencies in the country and their impact is also one of the recommendations of the study.

I hope the book would be liked by all sections of society including researchers, academicians, policy planners, journalists, historians and many alike.

Also whatever the shortcomings and lacunae in the book would be brought to the notice of the author and publisher for their rectification in subsequent edition.

Dr. Ahsanul Haq Chishti

CHAPTER – ONE

Introduction

The last decade of the 20th century could well be described as the decade of satellite television in India. The television boom began with a proliferation of, first local cable transmissions and later, satellite channels. CNN and STAR TV led the 'satellite invasion' from the skies, but it was not before too long that Indian language channels launched by Indian entrepreneurs also made their mark. Further, mainstream newspaper and magazine publishers such as Times Group of Bennett Coleman & Co. Ltd. (BCCL), the Living Media India Ltd. (LMI), owners of India Today Group and the *Eenadu* Group (Hyderabad) were writing their success stories in fields like recorded music, cable, FM broadcasting, film and television production business besides news and current affairs.

Many media houses like the India Today Group and the Jagran Prakashan Group entered tie-ups with foreign media houses and foreign media giants like CNN and Reuters are already tied up with Indian companies like TV 18 and the BCCL. Even Reliance is fast emerging as a big media giant in the country and companies have now presence across several segments of the media and entertainment industry, signaling the dawn of a new genre of media companies in India, billed as 'Media Conglomerate', similar to the likes of global companies like AT&T, Walt Disney, Time Warner etc. *(FICCI-PwC Report: 2006).*

However, it seemed more than a mere coincidence that this proliferation in transnational satellite television in India happened almost at the time when the country was opening up its economy to foreign investment and initiating a national policy of economic liberalization at the insistence of the World Bank and other international financial institutions. This brings home the fact that while the Indian economy was reforming itself to cope up with the demands of a global scenario; Indian media too was witnessing dramatic changes.

But economics alone was not the driving force behind the changes taking place in the Indian media industry. Political forces were equally responsible in quickening the pace of the change. The growing proximity between politicians and media groups became more and more evident and profound, though expressions of support for particular ideologies remained subtle. Also, coming to fore were the increasing levels, extent and modes of, financing by political groups. Examples are many, like Sun TV (promoted by Maran brothers), Jaya TV (promoted by AIADMK), Kalaignar TV (owned by family of M. Karunanidhi) and Makkal TV (identified with PMK) in Tamil Nadu, Kasturi TV (promoted by H D Kumaraswamy) in Karnataka, Kairali TV (CPI (M)'s Malyalam channel) in Kerala and Aakash Bangla and Chobbish Ghanta (Pro-CPI (M) channel) in West Bengal etc.

With the growth and rise of the media groups in the post-liberalisation India, the influence, reach and extent of these groups increased manifold. But with it the message also underwent a radical transformation. News, which was considered as something sacred, became a commodity to be sold in the marketplace. This had its impact on all the visible spheres of the public domain viz. political, economic and social.

When this media expansion process paced up further the Indian Government was taken by surprise. Starting in 1992, following the coverage of Gulf war of 1991, the cable invasion of India was met with unusual response from the public. It was a situation wherein both the Government and the Indian media industry were caught off guard.

As such the opinion got divided on almost expected lines. While the groups like BCCL and LMI welcomed the changes in the regulations on the entry of foreign media (both groups having tie ups with *Reuters* and *Daily Mail,* London respectively), papers like *The Hindu* and *The Indian Express* (both catering to the indigenous sentiments) criticized it. But with it emerged a third opinion, that of limited entry and limited restrictions. This view gained ground gradually.

Ownership and Monopoly

Democracy is defined as a Government by debate and discussion as against arbitrary diktats. For debate it is necessary to give information from diverse sources. Hence, plurality of sources of information is a must for democratic governance and debate. The growing tendency towards monopoly in the media which indeed is a result of commercialization and philosophy of business ought, therefore, to be a cause of concern for every democrat.

Once the business bug bites the media, it has to care for the market realities and adopt a strategy of market-oriented growth. Monopoly over information, whether of private individuals and institutions, or of the Government is detrimental to the democracy, for it may disseminate only one sided information and endanger fairness and objectivity. The corporate sector has entered the press mainly to do business like any other business to earn profit. *The Times of India* has, every morning, written above its masthead, "Made in ... (Name of the city)", signaling the commoditization of the news media.

The corporate sector has invariably its other businesses to safeguard and promote, and it has entered the press (and also the electronic media like television) to use its power to further its other business interests. The media thus becomes business oriented rather than people oriented.

While profits are necessary to enable the media to survive, to technologically upgrade itself and to be independent, it cannot be the dominant objective of the media, which has to be distinguished from other businesses. To inform and educate the people fairly, objectively and adequately, to enable them to discharge their role as citizens effectively, to act as watchdog of the interests of the society, to act as a forum of public grievances, to protect and promote the intellectual, mental and moral health of the society and to safeguard and enrich the cultural heritage of the society are, among others, important primary functions of the media which are, as it seems, irrelevant to the general business ethos.

It is relevant to quote here excerpts from an address delivered by Amartya Sen, celebrated Indian economist and Nobel Laureate on *Press Freedom and Development* at the General Assembly of the International Press Institute at New Delhi on January 29, 2001.

> "It is useful in this context to invoke the idea of what John Kenneth Galbraith has called 'countervailing powers'. What is needed is not so much to obliterate any particular power, but to confront one power with another. In the present context, this would be an argument not only for the multiplicity of private ownership from different parts of the business world, but also for supplementing them with-co-operative ownership as well as with ownership by independent bodies and statutory boards. The presence of other media, other than newspapers, including radio, television, the Internet etc. can also greatly help coverage and diversity. We have to rely, to a great extent, on the countervailing power of competition and confrontation to overcome the power of bias" (*Press Council of India Report: 2001*).

It will also not be out of place to quote here what E B White in a letter of W B Jones, January 30, 1976, in *Letters of E B White, Ed. Dorothy Lobrano Guth, 1976* wrote, inter alia, as follows:

"The press in our free country is reliable and useful not because of its good character but because of its great diversity. As long as there are many owners, each pursuing their own brand of truth, we the people have the opportunity to arrive at the truth. The multiplicity of ownership is crucial. It's only when there are few owners, or, as in Government-controlled press, one owner, that the truth becomes elusive and the light fails"*(Guth: 1976)*.

To save democracy, it is necessary that the concentration in ownership of the media is strictly regulated and media plurality and diversity of ownership structure is actively promoted. For a free media to exist, its ownership has to be diffused. Several devices may be thought of for the purpose; companies with distributed shareholdings and a limit on individual holdings, cooperative societies of journalists and others with similar distribution of shares, trusts with apolitical trustees and so on. A structure of ownership where the insiders in the media establishment are the majority shareholders has been in vogue in some countries with perceptible success. Some examples of newspapers owned by its employees are *Le Canard Enchaine* (Weekly, France), *Le Monde* (France), *The Journal Sentinel* (Wisconsin, USA), *The Journal Star* (Illinois, USA), *Feral Tribune* (Croatia) and *Nihon Keizai Shimbun* (Japan). There are also other newspapers where the employees own a sizeable amount of share holding of the stocks *(PCI Report: 2001)*. In India, similarly, the examples set by organizations like *Tehelka, Covert* and *NDTV* need to be studied in similar perspective.

Irrespective of the pattern of its ownership whether linked to large industrial houses or otherwise, a big newspaper generally expands its circulation by launching new papers or editions from new centres, often satellite editions. The term 'monopoly' is used here to signify sales of one particular newspaper in a preponderating majority of the total sales of all papers and to the practical exclusion of other papers. Such a monopoly may exist locally, in a particular city or town, or in a particular language where one paper may command such a large proportion of sales that it may be considered to have a monopoly.

Monopolies can arise also from the concentration of ownership and control of a number of newspapers in the hands of one owner or group. Establishment of a media outlet, whether print or electronic, is every day becoming more and more capital intensive. Only those who can command and deploy sizable resources can afford to start new media outlets, and withstand the competition from others. The result has been the takeover and closure of the financially and technologically weaker units and the growth of monopolies. This is a worldwide phenomenon *(Press Council of India Report: 2001)*.

The third Royal Commission on the Press in England in 1977 said that a monopoly publisher would determine what should be criticized and what should be investigated and that a journalist who did not conform to the policies of the monopolist would have either to compromise or quit. The *Monopolies and Mergers* legislation makes the consent of the Secretary of State obligatory whenever the controlling interests in a daily, Sunday or local newspaper are sought to be transferred to a person with other newspaper interests, if such a person already controls or would control after such a transfer, 25 percent or more of the voting shares of any other daily, Sunday or local newspaper having an average daily circulation of 5, 00,000 copies or more *(UK 2003:2004, www. opsi.gov.uk/acts/acts2003/ukpga_20030021_en_1:2005)*.

Growth of newspaper chains has been a major element in the 20th century journalism. The 20 largest newspaper companies account for almost half the daily circulation in the United States with more than 30 million of the 62 million copies sold each day. Also just six companies supply about 90% of world's media content all across the globe. This is roughly what emerges out of a global situation on media ownership. 98% of US cities today have only one newspaper publisher without any competition. Some newspaper publishers own radio and television stations, often in the same cities where their papers are published *(Padgaonkar: 2007)*.

The anti-monopoly laws directed against restrictive and monopolistic practices in trade and commerce have been applied to newspapers as well. In the famous *Associated Press vs. US* case, the US Supreme Court has held that anti-trust laws did not conflict with the freedom of the Press guaranteed by the First Amendment as that freedom does not confer the freedom to combine or keep out others from publishing newspapers. The Federal Communications Commission (FCC) has imposed restrictions on newspapers acquiring radio and television stations in the same city *(Bowker: 2003)*.

Over the last few decades, Canadians have debated what checks should be put on the power of media monopolies. Two Royal Commissions - the 1970 Davey Commission and the 1980 Kent Commission - have looked into the issue. The Commissions asked questions such as: Is there a connection between chain ownership and declining news coverage, how much influence do owners exert over programming? Does competition make a difference to the quality of coverage? And, should the Government regulate media ownership? *(PCI Report: 2001)*.

These are also the questions as relevant, directly or indirectly, to the emerging media scenario in India as they are elsewhere in the world.

CHAPTER – TWO

Cross Media Ownership: Political-Economic Perspective

What is the influence of media ownership concentration on democracy and debate? Is there a need to regulate media ownership and how much influence do owners exert over programming? Before going into the depth of all these issues and seeking answers, it is necessary to understand what we mean by Cross Media Ownership and what the current status of the term is, practically.

Cross ownership, by definition, is a method of reinforcing business relationships by owning stock in the companies with which a given company does business. In the US it also refers to a type of investment in different mass-media properties in one market. Cross media ownership also refers to a type of media ownership in which one type of communications (say a newspaper) owns or is the sister company of another type of medium (such as a radio or TV station)*(http://en.wikipedia.org/wiki/Cross_ownership: 2006, TRAI Consultative Paper: 2013).*

Cross Media Ownership has not remained limited to print and electronic media only. It has spread to diverse fields like the Internet, cable, recorded music, telecommunications, gaming, education and cinema as well. Times' ownership of WQXR Radio and the *Chicago Tribune*'s similar relationship with WGN Radio and Television are two examples of Cross media Ownership. Back home, *India Today* and *The Times* group are the two classic examples in this regard. While the former is now into print (*India Today, Mail Today, Cosmopolitan* etc.), television (*AajTak, Headlines Today*), FM radio, online, music (Music Today) and events (*India Today Conclave*), the latter is into, besides print editions of various publications like *The Times of India, The Economic Times, Femina, Filmfare* etc., entertainment television(*Zoom TV*), music(Times Music), radio, television news (*Times NOW*) and internet(*indiatimes.com*) as well.

Similar examples are from ZEE TV and Sahara Group. ZEE, which started with a television channel, has now 15 channels besides foraying into education (Zee Education), news, music and lifestyle besides DTH and gaming as well. On a similar pattern are the operations of Sahara Group ranging from television, print, and construction to fund management.

Theoretically, there are four types of media ownership: chain, cross media, vertical and conglomerate integration. Chain ownership is a situation where a newspaper company owns several publications in a country. Cross media ownership refers to common control over different media genres. It indicates the extent to which inter-media competition thrives or is restricted. Vertical integration suggests a setup where a company has stakes in various industries that go into producing the cultural product – say a newspaper company also owns large forests that provide paper pulp. Conglomerate ownership, the term used to describe a large company that consists of sections of often seemingly unrelated businesses. In such a setup there will be interlocking of directorship – where the media company would merely be used to exercise social and political influence on the decision-makers *(Madhav: 2008).* However, practically in India, one sees a mix of all the four types of ownership accumulation on the ground.

The worrying development is the Cross Media Ownership in which informatics, the press, radio and television, etc. sharing the same technology and content inputs, that are dependent on heavy capital resources, can become components of one gigantic publicity machine. A story carried in *Times Now* is flashed in the next day's *The Times of India* prominently. An interview of superstar Amitabh Bachchan by Arnab Goswami for *Times Now* was not only reproduced by *The Times of India* the next day but readers were also informed about the telecast timing of the programme well in advance *(Report, The Times of India: June 08, 2008)*.

Similarly, India Today also carries transcripts of many of AajTak programmes or India Today Conclave proceedings.

One school of thought is of the opinion that Cross Media Ownership should be allowed to expand uninterruptedly. Disallowing a newspaper house to invest in television or radio would be as ridiculous as not allowing a cycle manufacturer to diversify into motorcycles, they contend *(Mullick: 1997)*.

However, another school of thought believes that by encroaching upon the corresponding territories, media barons may exploit and thus tailor the views, comments and even news. That public is deprived of the plurality and diversity of news, views and information, they contend. Hence, curbs like limiting the equity of a media group to a quantifiable level in the other medium as has been proposed by the Government in the Indian Broadcast Bill and its earlier versions.

There is yet another opinion. That of 'synergic alliance', i.e. equity participation in the shape of Foreign Direct Investment (FDI) should be allowed to break or halt the growing monopoly of a few media giants in India who offer uneven level play and unhealthy competition to small and medium players. This opinion is based on the argument that if FDI can be allowed in core sectors like defence production or Atomic energy there should not be any objection to allow it in the field of media, which, undoubtedly, needs funds for modernization.

In this regard, so far the Government has allowed FDI in almost every segment of media with varying equity caps. As a result the I& B Ministry has cleared many projects so far *(Swarup: 2007)*.

Also companies like NDTV and Zee Telefilms have listed themselves with stock exchanges to go for public funds *(PCI Annual Report: 2007)*.

As such all these divergences of the problem and, more importantly, the likely impact it has had all through its short history impels one to undertake a study on the pros and cons of the Cross Media Ownership, and on the emerging related trends in the field. It makes it all the more important when even the Government (of India) is yet to have a draft policy on the issue.

Media Ownership - The Shrinking Base

While there are many more channels available today for the transmission of information and entertainment than in the past, there are fewer controllers of those channels. In the United States, in 1982 some 50 corporations, mostly US-based, controlled half or more of media business. In 1986 that number dropped to 29 and by 2002 it was just nine. Today, just four companies-Comcast, Walt Disney, 21st Century Fox/NewsCorp and Time Warner Holdings-control nearly 90% of the US media. Global Media czar Rupert Murdoch has reportedly predicted that eventually there will be just three global media giants and that his company will be one of them *(outlookindia. com: 2014, indiatogether.org:2007).*

In Britain between 1969 and 1986 nine multinational corporations purchased between them over 200 newspapers and magazines with a total circulation of 46 million copies. Today three companies-News UK, Daily Mail General Trust and Trinity Mirror-control 70% of national newspaper circulation. Just six companies, at present, supply about 90% of world's media content *(outlookindia.com: 2014, Padgaonkar: 2007).*

That possibly gives an idea of the pace of consolidation of media ownership in the world.

In Australia, in 1989, two men - Rupert Murdoch and Kerry Packer controlled 84 percent of sales of the 30 best-selling magazines. As the 1990s progressed, Murdoch came to control 63 percent of the metropolitan paper circulation. The trend has shown an even steeper upward curve in the mid and late 1990s with the Murdoch's *News Corporation* spearheading satellite transmission, through *Sky TV* in Europe and *Star TV* in Asia, at a staggering pace and Governments lack the will to influence and control it *(Padgaonkar: 2007, PCI Report: 2001).*

Media moguls in the 1990s never had it so good. Murdoch in Australia, Britain and the US, Silvio Berlusconi in Italy, Reinhard Mohn in Germany, Ted Turner (of CNN), Henry Luce and the Warner Brothers - Harry and Jack - in America. These big guns have built global empires of news transmission and entertainment that, some political economists like Ben Bagdikian, Robert McChesney, Dan Schiller and others fear, might become empires of the mind.

The rise of a global corporate media oligopoly, write Dan Schiller and Robert McChesney in the report for United Nations Research Institute for

Social Development (UNRISD: 2005), has two distinct but related facets. First, it means the dominant companies - roughly one-half US-based, but all with significant US operations - are moving across the planet at breakneck speed. Second, consolidation within and across each and every market segment is the order of the day. As local and regional media markets develop, specific companies - in many cases new ones, built up around privatized broadcast systems or constituted around new media - began to link up rapidly with one or another of a few emergent global giants. In each industrial niche, in turn, concentration duly increased, even as new subsidiaries of huge global media conglomerates continued to form *(robertmcchesney.com:2006)*.

The logic guiding media firms in all of this was clear - get very big very quickly, or get swallowed up by someone else - just as it was in many other industries. Among these, few global media firms own the major US film studios; the US television networks; 80-85 per cent of the global music market; the majority of satellite broadcasting worldwide; all or part of a majority of cable broadcasting systems; a significant percentage of book publishing and commercial magazine publishing; all or part of most of the commercial cable TV channels in the US and worldwide; a significant portion of European terrestrial television; and on and on and on *(ibid.)*.

Christopher Browne in *The Prying Game: The Sex, Sleaze and Scandals of Fleet Street and the Media Mafia* calls Rupert Murdoch "perhaps the most ruthless predator in history of the world news media"*(Browne: 1996)*.

Rupert Murdoch's News Corporation, though it lags behind some of its rivals in revenues, may be the most aggressive global trailblazer, but cases also could be made for several of the others. Murdoch spun off Sky Global Networks in 2000, consolidating his satellite television services that run from Asia to Europe to Latin America *(Goldsmith, Dawtrey: 2000)*.

Murdoch's Star TV dominates Asia. News Corporation's television service for China, Phoenix TV, in which it has a 45 per cent stake, reached 45 million homes in 2000 and enjoyed an 80 per cent increase in advertising revenues (admittedly from a small base) over the previous year. And this barely begins to describe News Corporation's entire portfolio of assets: Twentieth Century Fox films, Fox TV network, HarperCollins publishers, television stations, MySpace.com, cable TV channels, magazines, over 175 newspapers, and professional sport teams and much more *(robertmcchesney.com:2006, indiatogether.org: 2007)*.

Certainly, Murdoch has proved himself something of a regulation-buster, rolling back Federal Communications Commission (FCC) controls in the US when it permitted him, in contravention of its own regulatory code, to run a broadcasting station and a newspaper in the same city. With his acquisition of the *20th Century Fox,* and the subsequent launching of the *Fox TV,* Murdoch became a mogul of Mister Universe proportions *(PCI Report: 2001).*

In 1988 the merger of the giant media groups, *Time* and *Warner,* created the World's biggest media corporation-*Time Warner* employing over 3,00,000 people. The company owns subsidiaries throughout the world. Its magazine readership is estimated to be some 120 million. This does not include the world of Disney-Disney land, Euro-Disney etc. The same seems to be getting repeated in our country with one media group dabbling in varied cross-territories of media *(ibid.).*

Consolidation within the global media system, says Dan Schiller, is linked strongly to reciprocal changes in the structure of world of advertising. Advertising is a business expense made preponderantly by the largest firms in the economy. A whopping three-quarter of global spending on advertising ends up in the pockets of a mere 20 media companies *(Report, The Economist: March 11, 2000).*

The great myth about modern proprietors is that their power is less than it used to be. The fiefdoms of Beaverbrook, Northcliffe and Hearst, often invoked as the zenith of proprietorial omnipotence, were in fact smaller by every criterion than the enormous, geographically diffused, multi-lingual empires of the latest newspaper tycoons. The great media empires spanning the world have subjugated more territory in a decade than Alexander the Great or Chengis Khan in a lifetime and funnelled responsibility for the dissemination of news into fewer and fewer hands *(Coleridge: 1993).*

Whether or not it sounds exaggerated, we might pause to consider the advantages media moguls of today have over their peers of the past. Today their territories are restricted by neither time nor space; the next conquest is only a click away.

Ownership concentration; the political cost

The issue of who owns the media, and how much of it, matters. Many media analysts and writers have focused their attention on the potential harms that may result from concentrated media ownership, including the abuse of political power by media owners or the under-representation of some significant viewpoints.

Rupert Murdoch has often been accused of using his media holdings to advance his political agenda. In 2003 all 175 of his newspapers reportedly supported the invasion of Iraq. Thanks to his frequent interactions with the then British Prime Minister Tony Blair in the lead-up to the war, he came to be known in political circles as "the 24th member of the (Blair) Cabinet" *(www. indiatogether.com:2010).*

Similarly but much earlier, the same Murdoch brought constitutional crisis leading to the dismissal of Prime Minister Gough Whitlam's Government in Australia in 1972 when the Government refused to grant Murdoch a licence to develop bauxite reserves in Western Australia. Murdoch said he could not longer support Whitlam in his newspapers because his Government was grossly inefficient. The climax came when the Opposition, which had a majority in the Senate, refused to vote funds. The Government machinery was brought to a standstill, and the Governor-General, Sir John Kerr, had to dismiss Whitlam *(Noorani: 2008).*

This shows how much of a need individuals and societies have for diverse and pluralistic media provisions as concentrations of media ownership narrow the range of voices that predominate in the media and consequently pose a threat to the interests of society.

The ostensible purpose of media ownership becoming increasingly consolidated by the day is to achieve synergy & economy of scale for commercial advantage. But does it end there? What about the impact on news reporting, especially editorial comments? And the marketing-led changes in consumption, which influence culture & local customs? Also the subtle but undesirable effects on the freedom of expression!

After all, press, radio & television influence & control the average persons' understanding of themselves & their environment.

Democracy, Pluralism and Media Concentration

Recognition of the need to safeguard pluralism has historically been the main reason for diffused ownership. Media ownership matters to society, not only because of the need of pluralism in a democracy, but also because ownership patterns may affect the way in which the media industry is able to manage the resources. Restrictions of ownership, for example, result in a duplication of resources, which prevents the industry from capitalising on all potential economies of scale.

The ways in which ownership patterns affect the economic strength and efficiency of the sector are not solely a matter of broad societal interest but are obviously of immense and particular concern to media firms *(Doyle: 2002)*.

Industrial or economic arguments favouring a more liberal approach towards concentrations of ownership seem to have become more influential in determining media ownership policies in UK and Europe since the early 1990s. The elevation of industrial interests may, at least in part, be attributed to technological mystique surrounding developments such as convergence and globalization *(McChesney: 2000)*.

But relatively little work has been done to quantify precisely what efficiency gains or other economic benefits or, indeed, what disadvantages greater concentrations of media ownership might bring about. Above all, ownership and control over the media raise special concerns that do not apply in the case of other sectors of industry. Media concentrations matter because, as exemplified in the notorious case of the Berlusconi media empire in Italy (Slovio Berlosconi, former Italian prime minister, owns three out of four television channels of the country and the fourth one is owned by a friend of him), media has the power to make or break political careers *(Quail: 1998)*. (The United Front Government in India fell in 1998 because of a story carried by *India Today,* a leading national newsmagazine of the country. The story was about indictment of DMK by the Commission of Inquiry probing the assassination of former Indian Prime Minister, Rajiv Gandhi) *(indiatogether. com:2007)*.

Control over a substantial share of the more popular avenues for dissemination of media content can, as politicians are well aware, confer very considerable influence on public opinion. So policies that affect media concentrations have very significant political and cultural as well as economic implications. As these policies undergo sweeping 'reforms' to cater to the perceived needs of an increasingly dynamic media and communications environment in the 21st century, it is important to question whether the structures we are left with adequately safeguard the need and constitutional guarantee of citizens for media plurality.

CHAPTER – THREE

Cross Media Holdings: A Global Overview

Having discussed the theoretic perspective of Cross Media Ownership, it sounds logical to look at many of the countries of the world for their laws on media, specifically laws relating to Cross Media holdings. The aim is to look for the relevance and coherence of these laws in an atmosphere of democracy and liberty.

A wave of concentration in several western European countries in the 1950s and 1960s stimulated research activities on the subject. Such research into media concentration paid particular attention to the number of independent titles, growth of newspaper groups and chains, especially where this led to local monopoly ownership in a single circulation area or to Cross Media Ownership. During the 1980s and early 1990s, the dimensions of media concentration grew both in terms of geographical scope and media fields affected (*Meier, Trappel: 1998*).

Evidence of national and transnational corporate expansion within Europe by European and US media suppliers is plentiful. The 'European' media market is comprised not of a unified or cross-integrated system of provision for a collective audience but of a somewhat notional or artificial aggregation of the markets of each individual member state.

Regulation of the media at the European level took off in 1989 with the adoption of the EU directive-*Television without Frontiers*-and the Council of Europe Convention on trans-border television. Since then new items have been added to this directive. Media concentration has been investigated and analysed since the end of 1992 as preparation for an EU directive and competition legislation has been put to the test in the media field. The planning of the information society of future has given rise to numerous Community-level initiatives, many of which touch upon the traditional media *(Hirsch, Peterson: 1998)*.

Thanks to global media magnate Rupert Murdoch, the expansion and diversification of the media is an international phenomenon now. A wide range of economic and commercial motives that apply to media proprietors everywhere fuels these concentration trends; be it United States, Australia or Europe. Consequently, many examples of mergers, acquisitions and other strategic alliances involving large media and communication firms are found in almost every country of the world. Issues surrounding convergence and concentration of media ownership have worked their way onto the national policy agenda in most European countries over recent years and have also captured the attention of European Union policy makers *(Doyle: 2002)*.

Media Ownership Policies across the Globe

Diversity or plurality of media as a legitimate goal for public policy has been widely exemplified across Europe and countries like United States and Japan as a majority of countries have enshrined policy measures to safeguard and promote media pluralism in their own domestic legislations *(Committee of Experts: 1997)*.

Like Britain, most member states of the European Union impose some special curbs on media ownership over and above the safeguards provided by domestic laws. These special measures reflect recognition of the unique role that a diverse and pluralistic system of media provision plays in sustaining cultural diversity, social cohesion and, above all, democracy.

It may not be possible to put together in this book media ownership restrictions of all the countries of the whole world. These laws or restrictions have come up individually under the jurisdiction of each nation state and in accordance with the specific needs and characteristics of each country's media market. So no uniformity of evolution, execution or implementation should be expected. Not only do upper limits on media and cross media ownership change from one country to another, but also even the basic approach towards media ownership regulation tends to differ.

Most nations in the world that have achieved independence in the last 50 years recall the role of their press in their freedom struggles. (In fact, some of these countries continue to favour their newspaper industry with sops and concessions even today).

Most democracies have some form of legislation pertaining to media consolidation. While some countries stress on fair competition as the purpose, others stress on regulating foreign control.

But Governments' real concern is, and must be, to ensure dissenting political viewpoints by making sure that privately owned media are not held by a single entity.

In order to ensure media diversity, limiting Cross Media Ownership within markets is among the major planks having been employed for regulation and law, whether it is U.S.A. or U.K., Italy or India. The other major plank is to prevent monopolistic control of a medium within a market and controlling foreign direct investment in media companies.

Adequate limits on Cross Media Ownership exist in countries like United States, England, Italy and Japan. So is the case with limiting monopolistic control over media ownership where sufficient regulations have been put into practice.

While some countries such as Britain, France and Germany have opted for a mechanistic mode of determining upper limits on ownership, others such as Sweden favour a public interest test approach, allowing each instance of concentrated ownership to be considered and dealt with on a case-by-case basis.

This mechanistic mode of determining upper limits on ownership represents the most widely adopted approach, but the basis for measurement of ownership varies.

In Germany and UK the basis for calculation of media market share is audiences but the benchmark adopted elsewhere (such as in Italy) sometimes involves shares of media revenue also *(Meier: 1998)*.

Legislation in 1990 in UK laid down rules enabling the ITC and Radio Authority to keep ownership of the broadcasting media widely spread and to prevent undue concentrations of single and Cross Media Ownership, in the broader public interest. The Broadcasting Act of 1996 relaxed those rules, both within and across different media sectors in order to reflect the needs and aspirations of the growing industry against the background of technological advancements by:

- Allowing greater cross-ownership between newspaper groups, television companies and radio stations, both at regional and national levels, and
- Establishing public interest criteria by which the regulatory authorities can assess and allow or disallow mergers or acquisitions among newspapers, television and radio companies.

The 1996 Act overturned the rule that no one company could own more than two of the ITV (Channel 3) licenses. A new limit was set whereby no company could control franchises covering more than 15 % of the total television audiences. Local newspapers with more than 50% market share may now own a local radio station, provided one other independent station already exists in the area.

Newspaper mergers and transfers are subject to the consent of the Secretary of State for Trade and Industry (where the total daily circulation of the paper in question is five lakhs or more) usually after reference to the Competition Commission *(UK-2003: 2004)*.

In France, rules exist which limit monomedia ownership in the television, radio and press sectors. These restrictions were, to some extent, relaxed in the mid 1990s when upper restrictions on permitted levels of shareholdings in television services were increased from 25 percent to 49 percent. At the same time, maximum audience thresholds for ownership of commercial radio broadcasting licences were also substantially increased *(CE: 1997)*.

Even so, a complex set of monomedia and cross media restrictions still applies in France and restrictions on foreign ownership prevent non nationals from owing more than 20 percent of any French newspaper publishing *(Doyle: 2002, CE: 1997)*.

19

Ownership of the press in France is limited by rules that prevent anyone from controlling titles that account for in excess of 30 percent of the daily newspaper market *(Meier, Trappel: 1998)*.

Likewise in Italy, the 1981 national legislation prevents any individual or company from controlling a market share of more than 20 percent of the national press or 50 percent in any given region.

Such limits are, in theory, all well and good but they have not always succeeded in preventing powerful empires from developing in the press sector. In France, for example, the four most important publishers of national dailies (Socpresse, Group Le Monde, SAIP and Group Les Echos) accounted for a combined market share of some 83 percent in 1995 *(Committee of Experts on Media Concentrations and Pluralism (MM-CM): 1997)*.

In the United States, a Federal Communications Commission (FCC) newspaper/broadcast cross-ownership restriction prohibits the same company from owning a newspaper and a broadcast station in the same market. An FCC restriction prevents the same company from owning a cable station and a broadcast TV station in the same market.

Cross ownership rules, such as these, were developed in order to prevent any single corporate entity from becoming too powerful within any community. By preventing companies from cross owning within the same markets, the FCC embraces and protects a specified minimum of diversity of ownership that is crucial to a functioning democracy *(www.democraticmedia.org/resources/reading_list/media_ownership:2006)*.

However, the FCC allowed Murdoch's News Corporation to acquire Chris-Craft television stations (in markets where it owns newspapers), by waiving the newspaper/broadcast rule.

On September 13, 2001, FCC launched a proceeding designed to eliminate or dramatically weaken two longstanding safeguards designed to ensure greater diversity of media ownership. These include the rule that limits some of the power of the largest cable companies (the cable ownership limit), and a safeguard that prevents one company from controlling both a newspaper and a television station in the same market (the newspaper/broadcast cross-ownership rule).

Germany also follows UK in the regulating media ownership. The statute law does not provide any upper limits of ownership. Instead, mergers and acquisitions involving print media publishers that exceed a certain level are notified to the competition authorities for investigation.

Under the country's Act against Restraints of Competition, the upper limit of combined turnover in case of newspapers and magazines has been reduced to DM 25 million per annum from the general slab of DM 500 million per annum.

However, the Federal Cartel Office, the nodal agency for regulating competition, has been criticized for being excessively non-interventionist and thus allowing highly concentrated levels of ownership to accumulate across the country's newspaper industry *(Humphreys: 1996)*.

Dritter Rundfunkstaatsvertrag –the Broadcasting Treaty which came into force since 1997 relaxed previous restrictions on ownership of broadcasting companies and changed the basis of these restrictions from number of services to the quantum of audience share. Individual companies would now control licences covering upto a 30% share of the German television audience *(CE: 1997)*.

Under the 'viewer share' model adopted, companies are prevented from controlling broadcasting or press interests that, in total, give the company a degree of influence equivalent to more than a 30 percent share of the television audience in the country. However, this regulatory structure 'allows three big players up to 30 percent (in practice Kirch, Bertelsmann and Public Broadcasting) with a remaining of a little more than 10 percent for different minority groups' *(Kleinwachter: 1998)*.

In Asia many of the nation states are in the initial stages of their statehood. So the media is also in the process of growth to gradually brace up to the emerging situations. However, in many established countries with booming economies like China, Japan, India etc. the question of Cross Media Ownership has come to fore with political and social consequences.

In Japan, there is a concept of delivery of honest and comprehensive news through public service. And this concept has not been diluted yet despite the best efforts of Rupert Murdoch & Co.

Compared to US and most European countries where the global media giants have virtually bulldozed the domestic laws governing media regulation, Japan's media industry has remained by and large stable over the last few decades. Japan's media was almost free from the effects of corporate media globalisation until 1990s when Rupert Murdoch's STAR TV came to the country. It bought twenty per cent stake in one of country's top television networks-TV Asahi, much to the shock and resentment of local media players. Consequently, it formed JskyB – the equivalent of the UK's hugely dominant BskyB.

But, within a year or so, Murdoch sold off his Asahi shares owing to stiff resistance from the Japanese media industry which had perceived it as an invasion of outside.

Although there are laws restricting Cross Media Ownership in the country, Japan's main newspaper groups hold a majority stake in their affiliated TV networks, partly through direct ownership and partly through various subsidiaries.

Similarly in China, foreign investment in country's media industry was banned in 2005 by the Chinese Government after a year long entry (2004-05) into the country during which the Government felt that such a move was fraught with serious political, cultural and social consequences on Chinese broadcasting *(Rao: 2006)*.

Though there are no statutory limits on media ownership in Ireland, but the Radio and Television Act of 1988 requires the regulatory authority for commercial broadcasting (the Independent Radio and Television Commission) to consider the desirability of allowing levels of control over the media while awarding radio broadcasting licences.

Similarly, there are no special rules which govern press ownership in the country. However, its distinct characteristics and the need for plurality of ownership were specifically acknowledged in a report to the Government from the Competitions and Mergers Review Group (CMRG) in 2000.

In Denmark, which interestingly favours cross ownership of media, the national broadcaster; TV2, which includes eight regional companies, is obliged to commission the major part of its programmes, with the exception of news, current affairs and sports, to independent production firms. According to the competition law of 1989 all agreements and decisions constituting dominant influences on a certain market are to be announced potentially or effectively. The companies from outside the media sector, with the exception of publishers, may not exert this influence over local radio or television stations *(Meier, Trappel: 1998)*.

In Switzerland, the applicants for radio and television licenses must either be of Swiss nationality or, in the case of a company must have a registered office in Switzerland. The applicants for licenses must prove their sound financial background and their conviction not to endanger the variety of choice and opinion before approval by the authority. The applicants have to commit to communicate prior to its effectuation any change in ownership structure or any transfer of the license to third party. He or she is to inform the authorities about the balance of programming, sponsoring and profits and so on. The authorities granting licenses can require a representative composition of the board and the implementation of an advisory programme commission *(ibid.)*.

In 1993 Austria introduced specific provisions on media ownership, The Austrian Regional Radio Act and later Cable and Satellite Act of 1997. These laws limit the participation of press owners to a maximum of 26 % of the share in a radio station and a cable/satellite broadcaster. Persons or companies holding more than 25% of share in the newspaper in question are taken into consideration. Political parties, state agents like universities and the public service broadcaster are exempted from applying for local radio licenses and cable and satellite television services.

In Spain Law 10/1988 provides that no natural or legal person can own more than 25% of the capital of a national radio or television programme. Participation is limited to one single channel per person or enterprise. Restrictions with print media are, however, rare. A similar 25% rule for television services was implemented in Portugal in 1990. In Norway the ownership participation of private channel; TV2 is limited to one-third of the capital per shareholder *(ibid.)*.

In Belgium, legal regulations tend rather to support than to limit the concentration process and to institutionalize monopolistic structures. In the Flanders region, a consortium of newspaper publishers was originally granted the exclusive license for private television, providing them with a monopoly for almost the entire advertising market *(ibid.)*.

Discrepancies in Regulation

Going through the regulations put in place on ownership concentrations across countries one finds disparities on the subject and wide differences in approaches taken towards media regulation in general. These divergences also reflect individual market situations and variations in the resource levels available to support a diverse media ownership base. But one thing is certainly common in all these case situations. And that is the calls for deregulation came from media industry itself since early 1990s in every such country. It shows a competitive impetus on the part of dominant local players in the media industries in such countries to participate in an ever-increasing international trend towards media concentration and Cross Media Ownership.

This trend of revision of media regulation started in Europe from Italy in the mid 1990s and France introduced relaxations on concentrations in ownership in the television and the radio sectors in 1994. Germany followed suit when it overhauled and deregulated domestic rules on Cross Media Ownership in 1997. The deregulation of anti concentration provisions in United States by the Telecommunications Act, 1996 further facilitated this trend.

In the United Kingdom, the Government undertook a substantial review of rules on television ownership and on cross ownership of press and broadcasting in the Broadcasting Act of 1996. Later, the Communications Act of 2003 further suggested deregulatory measures like scrapping rules like preventing single ownership of ITV and more than one national commercial radio license, not allowing any newspaper group with over 20 % of the national market a significant stake in ITV and the introduction of a scheme to ensure that at least three commercial local or regional media voices exist in addition to the BBC in almost every local community *(UK-2003: 2004)*.

What it reflects is not a generalized, pan continental policy view on the subject but a mere patchwork of regulations, partly dictated by domestic circumstances to accommodate local industry interests. This has led to concerns, may be genuine, that these regulatory disparities obstruct cross national investment in media industry, at least in Europe and the emanating threat to pluralism with the growth of national and transnational European media conglomerates such as News International, Bertelsmann, Hachette or Fininvest. These concerns have brought media ownership regulation onto the pan European policy agenda.

Conventional modes of media production have been overtaken by developments surrounding digitization, convergence and the growth of the Internet and national policy makers had to respond accordingly while framing the laws on media regulation.

The advances in communication technologies have not come without concerns. One of the key concerns expressed is the potential for new patterns of cross-sectoral and/or vertical control to limit points of access to the media. Regulating 'gateways' and potential bottlenecks (e.g. monopoly control over conditional access systems, uplinking and downlinking of satellite channels, or user navigation systems or key content) has become pivotal to the objective of ensuring open and diverse systems of media provisions. Imposing restrictions on ownership too early on emerging media might deter investment and so prove counter-productive in terms of promoting diversity.

But contrarily, the competition based policy approach, with its emphasis on behavioural rather than structural interventions, has provided national regulators with an ideal alternative framework for dealing with gateways and bottlenecks. So, adopting this approach – where regulation aims to reduce the possibility of abuses of a dominant position rather than to eliminate positions of dominance – many European countries, including the UK, have recently begun to place more emphasis on the need for national competition authorities to enforce 'open' technological standards and to provide safeguards for all access points to the media.

To check ownership concentrations in media, many countries have toyed with the idea of providing subsidies to media organizations or media output that serve minorities to add to the diversity and range of 'voices' in the media. Some countries provide direct subsidies to promote diversity in the print media. Sweden, for example, provides direct subsidies to newspapers that occupy a weak market position. In Norway too, financial support is available to less popular daily newspapers, support is also given to certain political, cultural and scientific magazines. In Belgium, the French language press is supported by funds contributed by the broadcasting sector and a portion of commercial advertising revenues has been set aside each year to provide subsidies for the Flemish press.

Some other countries offer sops to broadcast services targeted at specific minority groups. In the UK, for example, the Welsh language television channel (S4C) relies heavily on a substantial public subsidy each year to stay in business and public funds are also available through the Gaelic Television Committee to finance Gaelic language programming broadcasts in Scotland *(Doyle: 2002).*

The Norwegian Example

Another method practiced to address the issue of media ownership concentration is to try to separate ownership from editorial control. Some countries have adopted 'editorial agreements' which seek to prevent proprietors from influencing the editorial content of the media products they own. The terms of such agreements between owners and editors vary from case to case and country to country and most are constituted on an informal or voluntary rather than a statutory basis.

Since 1953 Norway has been experimenting with this idea and for the most part it appears to have met with success in securing the independence of editors to take the lead on all day to day editorial decisions, free of interference from the owners. The terms of Norway's Declaration of Rights and Duties of the Editor, agreed to by both editors and publishers, not only give the editor "full freedom to shape the opinion of the paper" but also require him or her to "promote an impartial and free exchange of information and opinion" and to "strive for what he/she feels serves the society better" *(Citation, Rights and Duties of the Editor, Association of Norwegian Editors: 1953).*

The interference by the owners in day to day editorial decisions can often be indirect as well as direct. So, in order for editorial agreements to work effectively, they need to take care of a number of elements. It is essential that media owners be prevented from literally dictating, prescribing, or otherwise directly interfering in editorial matters on almost daily basis. Media owners also need to be restrained from pestering or intimidating editors and journalists into adopting certain viewpoints or ignoring others which otherwise they won't be doing.

The issue of crucial importance which comes to fore here is the appointment, dismissal and replacement of editors, CEOs or other key personnel in a media outlet. An owner's power to threaten dismissal or to select new appointees who share a similar outlook can be used to reshape editorial policy without the need ever to interfere directly with content. Such powers can be, and are, used to establish an unhealthy culture of obedience and self-censorship. Additional powers may lie in an owner's control over all major managerial decisions (including such issues as outsourcing of stories or consolidation or sharing of journalistic resources with other products etc.).

The range of strategies through which a determined media proprietor can exert influence over the content of the products he or she owns is so extensive as to make it virtually impossible for any editorial agreement to fully guarantee the independence of editors and journalists. For this reason, editorial agreements do not entirely dispense with the need for diverse media ownership. Nonetheless, as is demonstrated by the experience of countries such as Norway, a carefully worded agreement backed by the force of law can offer high levels of protection for editorial independence.

Another important means to ensure diversity and pluralism within media industry comes in the form of each country's continued support and commitment to maintain a national public service broadcasting entity. However, a competing market driven media economy dominated by commercial interests cannot be expected to encourage and promote such an idea which is essential for the preservation of pluralism. This is in addition to the fact that continued suppressive and bureaucratic control of the Governments over the state run broadcasters has led to their losing creativity, editorial choice and consequently audience. This coupled with the growth of private broadcasters and coming of satellite television, has led to people running away from the state run broadcasters thus leaving them to grapple for survival.

For example in South Asia, National broadcasters in a majority of countries are losing audience at a fast pace to either private media companies or satellite television companies from outside the region like STAR. Some smaller countries like Maldives or Bhutan fear the media from big countries like India.

Such policy interventions as limits on ownership control, press subsidies and editorial agreements have helped reinforce diversity and pluralism within the commercial media sector across the globe to a reasonable level. But additionally, it is equally encouraging to note to what extent public funded non commercial broadcasting organizations which are wholly dedicated to providing a range and diversity of high quality programming, as well as ensuring accurate and impartial news coverage and are committed to the principles of universal provisions, also help to ensure media pluralism.

With a global perspective on media policies now in mind, it would be interestingly essential to know about the ownership concentration scenario in India with its manifestations, consequences and impact on the society and evolution of the necessary relevant laws in the country including the Broadcast Bill.

CHAPTER – FOUR

National Media Policy—
Evolution of the Broadcast Bill

After going through the laws regulating media ownership in a majority of countries in the world, one way or the other, it is quite logical to have a look at the Indian Media laws or Media policy, to be specific, as being practiced on date. But do we have a media policy at all? The answer is no. There is no specific and comprehensive national media policy in vogue in the country since its birth some six decades ago. There are some guidelines and codes in case of television and cable, a cabinet decision (now almost reversed) in case of foreign investment in media, a censor board of film certification (known much for generating controversies than regulating content) for cinema and a Government nominated Press Council of India which also has not been able to register its presence.

This situation even led the judiciary to intervene in 1995 in *Cricket Association of Bengal vs Union of India* case followed by a Supreme Court observation and the Delhi High Court seeking an assurance from the Government on the subject. But even after the passage of 20 years that proactive piece of legislation on media is still awaited.

But does the situation warrant any laws or it was so sudden that the need for a law was felt now?

During the early years of independence while broadcasting remained a state monopoly the press was privately owned. Some concern was expressed even at that time about ownership of the press by big business houses. It was felt that the tendency would be to protect their own business interests first than show regard for objectivity and balance. In recent years scholars have shown concern over growing monopolies. Even as the numbers of newspapers in India have increased they are owned by fewer and fewer number of proprietors leading to increasing concentration of media ownership, though with increased circulation, reach and ad revenue *(Karkaria: 2004, Jeffrey: 2001)*.

In the advertising world too the consolidation among the front-runner companies has been at its peak *(Thomas: 2004)*. The report of the eighth PricewaterhouseCoopers (PwC) Global Entertainment and Media Outlook (January 2, 2008) has ranked India as the fastest growing market in the world for ad spends in entertainment and media in the next five years *(Kumari: 2008)*.

At present there are *Hindustan Thompson Associates* (HTA), *Mudra Communications Ltd.*, *McCann-Erickson India Ltd*, *Ogilvy & Mather Ltd.* and *Rediffusion –DY&R,* a blend of local and multinational agencies working as major players in this Rs. 47, 500 crore industry. The world's largest agglomeration, the US $ 40 billion *Interpublic Group,* plans to consolidate the buying power of all its Indian agencies with an integrated media service unit called Magna Global which will represent the aggregate media negotiating interests of *Interpublic's* Indian entities *(FICCI-KPMG: 2016, Kohli: 2005)*.

Given such developments, it would seem likely, that before too long, media buying power in India will be in the hands of two major players, each sharing a substantial transnational base, along with three smaller groups *(Thomas: 2004)*.

In this context to argue that the ownership of Indian media is relatively diverse seems somewhat untenable. From the 1950s critics constantly argued that Indian newspapers were largely controlled by "monopoly capitalists". In 1954 the First Press Commission contended that the power of the holder of a monopoly to influence his public in any way he chooses should be regulated and restrained *(Jeffrey: 2001, First Press Commission Report: 1954)*.

Eleven years later, the Inquiry Committee on Small Newspapers urged "maintaining (the) outcry against the growth of newspaper chains". In 1973 the Indian Federation of Working Journalists decried "the vested interests of the monopoly houses which own the biggest newspapers with the biggest circulations" *(Indian Federation of Working Journalists (IFWJ): 1974, Jeffrey: 2001)*.

In the early 1980s veteran journalist Pran Chopra argued that concentration of ownership was growing. And a report written for the Second Press Commission in 1982 advocated public takeover of the top eight newspaper establishments to delink the press from the monopoly Houses" *(Noorani: 2008, Jeffrey: 2001, PCI Report: 2001)*.

The picture of the Indian press as it emerged from the report of the First Press Commission, which was as judiciously worded as a judgment, caused concern. Of a total of 330 dailies, five owners controlled 29 newspapers and 31.2% of the circulation, while 15 owners controlled 54 newspapers and 50.1 % circulation *(PCI Report: 2001)*.

The early preoccupation of Indian Governments and politicians with "monopoly house" control of newspapers was reflected in the annual reports of the Registrar of Newspapers in India (RNI). At the start in 1956, "many publishers...did not disclose effective common ownership," the then Registrar had noted. But "on the basis of further information collected during 1957 ... a large number of groups and multiple units came to notice". *Press in India,* as the Registrar's reports came to be called later, each year contained a chapter compiling statistics on ownership. Changing little over forty years, the chapter listed owners who published more than one title-135 in 1955 and 142 in 1995 comprising 810 news and non-news interest newspapers. The figure rose to 504 units comprising 2006 news and non-news interest newspapers during 2006-07 which further escalated to 2268 units comprising 8203 news and non-news interest newspapers in 2014-15*(RNI Annual Reports: 2007, 2014-15, Jeffrey: 2001)*.

It won't be out of place here to take a look at the ownership pattern as emerging on the ground by analyzing the findings of the latest RNI report, released for the year 2014-15(59th Annual Report) for the purpose of understanding the problem of media ownership as it is evolving in the country.

Pattern of ownership in Indian Media

The office of Registrar of Newspapers of India (RNI) is the nodal agency for registration of publication titles in every category in the country. The figures released by this agency in the form of its annual reports give a reflection of the trend or pattern evolving on the ground.

The report for the year 2014-15 reveals that individuals owned a majority of publication titles in India. Out of 22,787 publications which furnished Annual Statements with RNI for the year under review, individuals owned 19, 765 (86.74 per cent), followed by Joint Stock Companies 2,099 (9.21 per cent), Societies and Associations 355 (1.56 per cent), Trusts 289 (1.27 per cent), Firms & Partnership 211 (0.93 per cent), etc. The remaining 17 publications were owned by other categories *(RNI, 59th Annual Report: 2014-15)*.

Periodicity-wise, among 7,905 dailies, bi and tri- weeklies 6,375 (80.65 per cent) were owned by Individuals, followed by Joint Stock Companies 1232 (15.59 per cent) and Firms and Partnerships 133 (1.68 per cent).

Individuals also owned a sizeable number of other periodicals. Weeklies and Fortnightlies owned by individuals were 7,582 (93.79 per cent) and 2,092 (94.28 per cent) respectively. Out of 3,912 Monthlies, 3,291 (84.13 per cent) belonged to Individuals and 292 (7.46 per cent) to Joint Stock Companies. Out of 76 Annuals, Joint Stock companies owned 32 (42 per cent) followed by individuals with 19 (25 per cent).

Language-wise, out of 12,516 Hindi publications, 11,692 (93.42 per cent) were owned by Individuals, followed by Joint Stock Companies, 558 (4.46 per cent) and Society and Association, 91 (0.73 per cent). In English, out of 2,219 publications, Individuals owned 1,251 (56.38 per cent) followed by Joint Stock companies 766 (34.52 per cent), Societies and Associations 98 (4.42 per cent). Individuals owned the maximum number of newspapers in all the languages except Malayalam in which Joint Stock Companies owned 114 (47.30 per cent) out of 241 titles. In Manipuri, Kashmiri, Bodo, Sindhi, Dogri and Santhali languages, Individuals owned 100 per cent publications.

State-wise, Uttar Pradesh and Delhi retained the 1st and 2nd positions in publishing the maximum number of publications respectively for the year under review. In Uttar Pradesh, out of 5,506 publications, 5,208 (94.59 per cent) were owned by Individuals and 185 (3.36 per cent) by Joint Stock Companies. Out of 2, 465 publications published from Delhi, Individuals owned 1900 (77.08

per cent) publications, followed by Joint Stock Companies 329 (13.35 per cent) and Society/Association 111 (4.50 per cent).

In all states Individuals owned the largest number of newspapers except Kerala and Goa where Joint Stock Companies owned 144 (48.32 per cent) out of 298 and 13 (61.90 per cent) out of 21 publications respectively. All the 11 publications brought out from Andaman & Nicobar Island and all 13 publications from Daman & Diu were owned by Individuals (*RNI, 59th Annual Report: 2014-15*).

Consequently, the circulation of publications, owned by individuals in 2014-15 was the highest with 36,59,42, 010 copies (71.68 per cent), followed by Joint Stock Companies 11,70,25,508 copies (22.92 per cent) and Firms and Partnerships had a circulation of 1, 16, 72,598 copies (2.29 per cent).

Societies and Associations owned publications circulated 70, 46, 727 copies (1.38 per cent), Trust-owned publications circulated 77, 65,075 copies (1.52 per cent), Government owned publications circulated 871890 copies (0.17 per cent) and those owned by others circulated 1, 97,637 copies (0.04 per cent).

Cross Ownership/Common Ownership, the RNI findings

As per the RNI study under evaluation, there were 2268 cross ownership or common ownership units (as the study used the term for) during 2014-15, which owned 7, 983 'news-interest' publications. Of these, 5, 322 were dailies and Tri/Bi-weeklies, 1805 weeklies and 856 of other periodicities. Out of 7, 983 such annual statements furnished with the RNI, 6, 437 belonged to Individuals, 1,295 to Joint Stock Companies, 107 to Firms and Partnerships, 74 to Trusts and 70 to other Units.

Apart from "News & Current Affairs" publications, says the report, these 2268 cross ownership/common ownership units also brought out 220 publications which had non- news content like specialty magazines. Thus, total media titles owned by these units were 7983 in number.

Out of this, dailies published by these units had a total circulation of 21, 61, 02, 937 copies per publishing day, i.e. 72.93 per cent of the total circulation of all dailies published in India *(ibid)*.

The circulation of publications, owned by Common Ownership Units during 2014-15 was 28, 21, 82,215 copies per publishing day i.e. 55.27 per cent of the total. Out of these, 'news-interest' publications circulated 27, 55,75, 069 copies and 'non-news-interest' publications circulated 66, 07,146 copies per publishing day.

Out of a total circulation of 27, 55,75, 069 copies per publishing day claimed by 'News & Current Affairs' publications in this category, 17,35,81,381 copies (62.99 per cent) were claimed by Individuals, followed by Joint Stock Companies 8,74,77,778 copies (31.74 per cent), Firms and Partnerships 74, 49, 471 copies (2.70 per cent), Trusts 45,49,397 copies (1.65 per cent) and Others 25,17,042 (0.91 per cent).

Cross Media Ownership:

History and Evolution of the Broadcast Bill

The problem of media concentration, as discussed earlier in the chapter, has been existent in the country since long and the relevant reports of Press Council, RNI and Ist and IInd Press Commissions give an idea of the heavy concentration in the Indian media. The freedom of press is not merely a professional right that involves journalists but an essential right of the readers to get fair, accurate, objective, balanced and truthful information. The control of the newspapers by big business results in the distortion of news and also in projecting the ideology of the owners of the newspapers.

Accordingly, the fact finding committee of the Press Commission in 1973 recommended that a person carrying on business of publishing a newspaper should not have an interest in any other business in excess of 10% of its subscribed share capital. Secondly, a person having an interest in any other business should not have, in the business of publishing a newspaper, an interest that is in excess of 10% interest. According to the Commission, such delinking and diffusion will not be violative of either article 19(1) (a) or 19(1) (g) of the Indian Constitution *(PCI Report: 2001, Goyal, Rao: 1981)*.

But with the onset of first phase of economic reforms in the country in 1990s, media too began expanding its operations and reach. With the opening of Indian skies to private broadcasters and increased cross media interests among media barons in the absence of any media policy regulation or law in the country, the problem assumed a serious dimension and for the first time it generated a public debate including intervention from the judiciary.

First Broadcast Bill

However, it was only in 1997 when the then Government rose to the occasion and the issue took a legislative shape with the preparation of a first ever draft Broadcast Bill by the then Information and Broadcasting minister, S. Jaipal Reddy. The bill, among other things, proposed a cap of 20% equity on cross media holdings in the country. However, the bill could not be taken up by the parliament as the Government of the day fell resulting into elections that brought in a BJP-led regime, which had a different set of priorities in media. But it did set in an enthusiastic debate on the pros and cons of cross media holdings in the country.

But much before the introduction of the Broadcast Bill, an eight-member parliamentary sub- committee, headed by Ram Vilas Paswan, had been constituted on March 30, 1994. This was following the recommendations made by the consultative committee attached to the Ministry of Information and Broadcasting *(Report, The Pioneer: March 30, 1996)*.

In its 104-page report that the committee submitted in March 1996, it made 46 recommendations encompassing almost all areas of media including cross ownership. The committee made a strong plea to put an end to cross media ownership in Indian media. "Care should be taken to prevent monopolies. Television programming should be more decentralised and five zones could be constituted as recommended by the Verghese Committee", the committee suggested *(Raman: 2008, Report, The Pioneer: March 30, 1996)*.

Following this, the Union cabinet started an exercise to prepare a draft bill to govern the broadcast companies in the country. A committee headed by the then Prime Minister broadly cleared the bill after a thorough review. It, however, framed a high power panel of Secretaries to deliberate on three contentious issues; Cross media holdings, Foreign Direct Investment (FDI) and equity share of advertising companies in broadcast companies *(Sinha: 1997, Swarup: 2007)*.

Initially the panel was of the opinion that cross media holdings in the Indian media should be put to an end. But subsequent pressures and hectic lobbying by media giants, including *Hindustan Times* and *The Times of India*, and political leaders of the ruling United Front, including a minister, led the panel to recommend otherwise. The particular minister had a stake in a Chennai based broadcast company, which was being promoted by a South based newspaper company. The panel of Secretaries, later submitting to the Prime Minister, recommended that cross holdings be allowed between broadcast and newspaper companies *(Report, Business Standard: February 22, 1997)*.

But Nitish Sengupta, then I&B Secretary and chairman, Sengupta Committee on Prasar Bharti Bill maintained that the checks on cross media holdings were necessary for a healthy media scenario. "The objective (behind the restrictions) is to prevent the same group of people controlling both print and electronic media. If the same people who control print media also branch off into electronic media and attempt to dominate it, it will not be healthy in the long run, he contended *(Uniyal: 1998)*.

In March 1997 the Union cabinet cleared the draft of the Broadcast Bill to be tabled in the next session of parliament. Among other things it proposed a cap of 20% on cross media ownership. A media company would not have more than 20% of equity share in any other branch of media if it ventures into that stream; the bill had proposed *(Report, Business Standard: April 30, 1997)*.

The bill, as written above, was to be tabled in the parliament in its next session. But during the time the United Front Government fell and a new alliance Government led by BJP came to power.

Again, the UPA in its first term also planned to introduce the bill (Broadcast Bill, 2007). The bill, in the present form which is its 19th amended version, has almost repeated the cross holding provisions of Broadcast Bill of 1997*(mib.nic. in/bills: 2008)*.

Better late than never before, as they say. It took the Government almost 12 years to come up with a draft broadcast bill about which every political party or formation had more or less similar opinion. It was only the pressure from the industry and operators that things got delayed. Otherwise, every political combination, left, BJP or Congress vowed to bring in legislation, set up a media policy framework and regulate the FDI, as is evident from their party perspectives on Media.

India's National Media Policy: Political Parties' Perspective

Indian polity in the current scenario is broadly divided into three groups of opinion, each led by BJP, Left and Congress on expected lines. As such these are the opinions shaping or influencing the policies of the Government of the day.

All these three groupings or political combinations framed their media policies which were reflective of their ideologies and predicaments of the given situations. Predicaments because foreign media or satellite television came to India not just because they wished so (rather despite their objections to the same), it just happened. Similarly allowing FDI in media was more out of the compulsive economic conditions of the day and pressures from the industry than a genuinely thought out policy initiative.

Here is a paraphrased account of the media policies of each of these political combines:

Left Parties

Left Parties, with CPI (M) as its dominant constituent, believe in strengthening the Prasar Bharati Corporation so that it becomes a genuine public broadcasting service.

The parties stand for prohibiting cross media ownership to prevent monopolies and ownership expansion of big media houses. They also demand reversal of the decision allowing foreign stakes of print media in the country *(Report, The Hindu: January 24, 2006).*

Among other things they demand the enforcement of a media code for satellite broadcasters and ensuring that states have a say in media policy and programmes in the public broadcasting service and all national languages listed in the Eighth Schedule of the Constitution are encouraged and developed.

The parties deem it necessary to codify the laws relating to legislative privilege to prevent any infringement of the freedom of expression of the media for which they expect the parliament and state legislatures to undertake the initiative *(cpim.org/search/node/Media%20Policies?page=1: 2007).*

Another major constituent of the Left, CPI is also against any raise in the FDI cap of 26 % in the country's media industry. With the ownership of media houses passing into the hands of large corporate entities, the party believes a further increase in the FDI would not be in the national interest. The party believes that news and views are not like any other commodity to be traded and the media had the power and capacity to condition the thinking of people and influence their opinions (*Report, The Hindu: January 24, 2006*).

The party is also against any dilution of the Union cabinet resolution of 1955 under which foreign news agencies are required to distribute their news in India through Indian news agencies. In fact, this resolution should be strengthened in the interest of domestic agencies, the party contends (*ibid.*).

CPI also demands the Government to initiate legislative measures to stop publication of foreign journals such as the *International Herald Tribune* in the country. The party also voices its opposition to increasing volume of syndicated material from abroad (*cpim.org/search/node/Media%20Policies?page=1: 2007*).

Congress

Congress party doesn't have any written media policy. Since the party has been in the Government most of the time, the policy adopted by the Government since independence largely reflects the party's policy as well. In this case reference is often made of 1955 union cabinet resolution restricting any foreign investment in print media in the country (*Tiwari: 2007*).

The party believes in a free and vibrant media which is necessary for a democracy. But, equally the party wants the same to come with some reasonable restrictions as envisaged by the first Information and Broadcasting Minister Sardar Vallabhbhai Patel. These restrictions include relationships with foreign media groups and their taking over of Indian media publications and news agencies (*Moily: 2008*).

The party claims to have dissuaded newspapers in India to take direct feeds from foreign agencies. This, the party believes, has helped home news agencies like the Press Trust of India and the United News of India or others to grow and stand to the competition at local and international level (*Tiwari: 2007*).

Bhartiya Janata Party (BJP)

The BJP stands to ensure that ownership of the media is in the hands of natural-born Indians only. While the party opines for a limited extent of 20 per cent foreign equity investment in the electronic media in view of its large capital requirements, the party is categorically against any investment in the other media, including the print media (*www.bjp.org*).

On the use of editorial matter from outside in electronic media, the BJP vows to ensure that the safeguards contained in Article 19 (2) of the Constitution are fully implemented to balance freedom and public interest.

To achieve this goal, the party intends to improve the provisions of the Prasar Bharati Act to let Prasar Bharati evolve as an effective public broadcasting system, which would be accountable to Parliament but free from Government control, immune from political influence but sensitive to the diverse needs of Indian society (*www.scatmag.com/govt.htm: 2007*).

The party would ensure and encourage the availability of a variety and plurality of views and diversity in programming by discouraging monopolies and maximizing the number of voices, which can use the mass media. It will, therefore, impose appropriate cross-media and cross-platform restrictions and also restriction on investment by media in cable cable-TV companies and vice-versa (*Party draft paper on the subject: 2007*).

While permitting, by license, the entry of private enterprise and investment in radio and television broadcasting, purely on commercially acceptable terms determined by bids, the party intends to ensure that the up linking of television programmes is from India and the foreign equity investment in audio-visual media is restricted to 20 per cent with management of all types of the media is in Indian hands (*ibid.*)

The party intends to facilitate the development of an efficient and competitive Indian broadcasting industry by providing a level playing field to the nascent Indian industry vis-a-vis a highly developed foreign-based broadcasting industry (*ibid.*).

Politics of the media apart, as the situation can be described, India's media policy, rather the lack of it, has evoked an interesting debate among media analysts, experts and general masses.

Cross Media Curbs—Diversity of Opinion

The subject has thrown open a serious debate to discuss the merits and demerits of cross media curbs.

No curbs

"Disallowing newspapers in television will restrict plurality and diversity of viewers' choice" is the general opinion propounded by the adherents of no-cross media curbs school of thought. Cross media curbs are unrealistic and against public sentiment, they believe *(Mullik: 1997)*. This opinion stresses against any regulation or restrictions on cross media holdings and believes that newspapers are better equipped to branch off into any other media stream, like television, than any other entrepreneur.

"The fear of monopoly in the Indian media marketplace appears unfounded, since it is quite vibrant and competitive. There are hundreds of newspapers in English, Hindi and other languages with substantial circulation. In Delhi alone, there are as many as 170 registered newspapers, out of which there are 12 English and 9 Hindi mainline newspapers", they maintain (*The Times of India: July 31, 1997*).

"The Indian media is responsible, self regulatory and self governing. There is no need for external censorship as a lot of self imposed restrictions already exists", believes Swati Chaturvedi, leading journalist and television host (*Chaturvedi: 2004*).

Similarly another argument this school of thought comes with is that a good part of the social role of radio and television is news and current affairs coverage in which newspapers have considerable expertise. To deny them opportunity for lateral expansion is like saying that cinema artists are automatically debarred from transferring their talents to the television screen. Nationwide, they say, Hindi newspapers which account for the single largest bloc of circulation still reach only 35 per cent of the total Indian market. No individual newspaper among them can enjoy an outsized share of the readership that is even more fragmented in case of other languages, including English (*Sarkar: 1997*).

On the technicalities of the issue, the relevance of the cross media curbs vis a vis technology also came to be questioned. "Significantly in the United

States and some other countries, satellite television, satellite radio, cable, DTH and MMDS (Microwave Multipoint Distribution System) are outside the purview of the cross media restrictions. Only terrestrial services are covered by cross media curbs, Mullick opined in the series of articles he wrote on the subject during 1997.

The Times of India conducted a survey in four cities of New Delhi, Mumbai, Kolkatta and Bangalore through a market research group Ess Pee Associates (EPA). With a sample size of 1023 respondents the survey had an equal representation of adult males and females in these four cities. According to the survey about 70 per cent of the respondents were against imposing any restrictions on print media's entry into broadcast business, 76 per cent felt newspapers were better equipped to run the television companies and 63 per cent felt newspapers should not be barred from entering the television business *(Report, The Times of India: July 31, Nov 8, 1997).*

Pro-curbs

As against this, the architects of the Broadcast Bill propound that allowing newspapers to diversify into other forms of electronic media would lead to their monopolising the entire market and audience to such an extent that public would be deprived of plurality and diversity of news, views and information *(Raman: 2008).*

In fact, the Supreme Court in 1995 clarified that such regulations will not imply any conflict with the constitutional provisions for freedom of speech and with the right of citizens to do "business" *(Rao: 1997).*

In a separate but concurring judgment, Justice Jeevan Reddy, one of the three judges of a constitutional bench of the apex court, which set the pace for subsequent developments in the broadcast scene in the country including the proposed Broadcast Bill, observed: "By manipulating news and disinformation, to suit their commercial or other interests, they would be harming and not serving the principles of plurality and diversity of views, news, ideas and opinions. Citizens should have the benefit of plurality of views and a range of opinions on all public issues *(Rao: 1997).*

"A successful democracy posits an aware citizenry. Diversity of opinion, views, ideas and ideologies is essential to enable citizens to arrive at informed judgment on all issues which can't be negated by a monopoly, whether the monopoly is of the state or any other individual, group or an organisation", the court observed.

And for this reason, as earlier discussed, came up the Broadcast Bill with cross media curbs to the tune of 20% of the total equity. The proposed bill did not disregard scope and strength of cross media as is often made out. The bill only sets certain limits on control, not on participation *(ibid.).*

As for the claim that cross media curbs were originally meant in United States for the single newspaper TV cities, Rao maintains that for whatever reason, historical or otherwise, there are certain cities and states (seven or eight) in India where a single newspaper dominates, in a couple of cases with more than 50% market share, both in circulation and readership as in the cases of Andhra Pradesh or Rajasthan. Hence, he contended, the scope for limiting cross media holdings *(ibid.).*

The question is not whether newspapers are better equipped or not to operate broadcast services, but what is good for the people and the country. Also it is not a question of business interests alone. The creativity and entrepreneurship potential in the country being what it is and the imbalance and inequalities in access to media being what they are, certain cross media regulations are more than desirable. Business interests of a couple of media barons will no doubt get affected because of such regulations. But a much larger number of people, readers as well as viewers, will eventually be the beneficiaries; so also the journalists and the democratic process and civil society *(Nathan: 2006).*

Implementation, the practical way

However on the question of implementation of the cross media curbs, various opinions and formulae were being expressed and debated. J D Agashe, a US based media analyst, recommended 3-slab cross media curbs based on a newspaper's market share in a particular city/town.

First, he suggests, there should be no equity curbs for newspapers with less than 33% market share in a particular city/town wanting to invest in a terrestrial news channel. Second, those newspapers whose market share falls between 34 and 49 per cent should be allowed to hold up to 49 per cent stake in a terrestrial news channel in the same city/town. No restrictions should be placed on TV stations outside that town.

Third, those newspapers whose market shares are 50 per cent and above, should not be allowed to hold more than 33 per cent stake in terrestrial news channel in the same town.

A sort of reciprocal arrangement, such an approach would safeguard the interests of small newspapers. For instance a newspaper whose circulation is just 1,000 should be allowed to invest freely in television instead of being restricted to 20 per cent or so equity, as per the provisos of the Broadcast Bill *(Agashe: 1997)*.

In the case of equity restriction, it is relatively easy to ask for disinvestments as and when a newspaper gets into broadcast service *(www.cmsindia.org/ roundtable, 2008)*.

Bhaskara Rao, founder Director, Centre for Media Studies, New Delhi, however, offered an alternative proposition. He suggested that instead of putting a restriction on equity participation for restraining media monopoly, it may be better to use the market share concept either in terms of circulation or readership or both *(Rao: 2006)*.

Whether one takes the equity or market share approach, either way it is complex to keep track of the composition of equity and market share and the changes therein. This calls for an effective monitoring mechanism with an independent regulatory authority. The authority would not only maintain the entire requisite database for the purpose but also play the role of a watchdog in the whole process, somewhat like Press Council and TRAI. That is also what formed the dominant part of the deliberations of the 26th meeting of State Information Ministers' Conference on Broadcast Bill at New Delhi *(SIMCON-XXVI: 2007)*.

Defending the 20% cross media curbs in the proposed Broadcast Bill, Rao observed that up to 5 per cent equity one could hold in inter and intra media services. Even in the case of newspapers, he says, the said bill does not discourage holding of up to 20 per cent equity of a broadcast service. In fact, the newspaper can also hold 5 per cent in more than one broadcast services. Control and participation, rightly, have not been mixed up. However, in reality, this may not prevent manipulative control of more than one media by the same entities.

But Dileep Padgaonkar, Chairman, Asia Pacific Communication Associates (APCA), is much more realistic on the issue when he agrees to a certain degree of cross media restrictions. Though Padgaonkar does not visualise a time when a real challenge on the issue is thrown up in the country and sees no reason comparing the US pattern with that of India. However, he does see an aggressive Murdochisation of the media going on *(Padgaonkar: 2007)*.

The opinions continue till date. But in the meantime, media in India continues to expand in the absence of any national media policy or any regulation. There are a number of definitive trends visible. These trends suggest the changing contours of the media industry in the country forcing the Government to change its policies from time to time. FDI is a case example.

CHAPTER – FIVE

Cross Media Ownership: Current Trends in India

In the absence of any national media policy the accumulation of ownership interests continues with consequences for the future. Cross media ownership, as some media house owners may say, may be in the initial phases of its impact in India but the trends owing their manifestations to the origin and practicality of the term are already much more pronounced on the ground in the country. These are in addition to the content channelisation and ownership shrinkage of the media outlets going on otherwise.

Here are some of the current trends obtaining in the media industry in India:

Foreign Direct Investment (FDI)

Almost reversing its 1955 cabinet decision barring any foreign investment in media, the Indian Government has thrown open all the splits of media; newspapers, television, advertising, films, radio etc. to foreign investment, though with varying equity caps. For example, it is 26% for news publications and 100 % for non-news publications, 100 % (with certain conditions) for television, 100 % for film production, 100 % for advertising, 20% for radio etc.

As a result, so far the I& B Ministry has cleared many titles in news and current affairs category, more than hundred scientific and technical titles and around two hundred Indian editions of foreign specialty publications for FDI. By the same day, many more titles in news and current affairs category, scientific and technical titles and Indian editions of foreign specialty publications were under the consideration of the Ministry for the same. Some of the key local groups in whose brands the FDI has been made include *Hindustan Times, India Today, Times Group, CNN-IBN, Jagran Prakashan, Business Standard* etc.*(Swarup: 2007, pib.nic.in/pressreleases: 2009).*

A Growing Digital Media

Over the past few years digital media has emerged as an important platform of communication. Digital marketers are recognising this trend and are now considering to or are already on their way to execute 'Mobile-first' branding and customer engagement strategies. An upswing in the advertising through this medium has been recorded by many surveys and studies.

In 2015, digital media rose by a significant 38.2% growth. Digital advertising, which was Rs.4, 350 crore in 2014, is projected to touch Rs. 8, 110 crore in 2016 *(FICCI-KPMG:2016).*

India has becomes the world's fastest growing smartphone market. Currently, the mobile phone subscriber base is almost nine times the installed base for PCs in India. By the end of 2014, the country had around 116 million Internet-enabled smartphones and the number is expected to reach 435 million by 2019*(livemint.com: 2015).*

With eyeballs shifting from print and television to online media, the second screen phenomenon has become a reality that cannot be ignored. This growth presents a good opportunity for digital content aggregators, advertisers, app developers and online streaming companies to engage users through relevant mobile-led strategies.

Google and Facebook account for close to half of the online advertising revenue in Asia, and the dominance can be attributed to their massive user base. The digital advertising is expected to grow at a staggering rate of 33.50 % to reach a whopping Rs. 25, 520 crore by 2020. Thus leaving behind conventional ad spending platforms like print (8.60%), television (15.0%), radio (16.9%) and OOH (13.1%)*(FICCI-KPMG:2014, 2015, 2016; bestmediainfo.com:2014).*

A booming advertising industry

India is going to be the fastest growing market in ad spending in coming years *(Kumari: 2008).* In addition there is a 100 per cent FDI provision in advertising in the country. This has led to a race for accumulation of interests and ownership in the ad spectrum as well.

Media boom in India is often being attributed to the flourishing advertising market in the country. Advertising sector which pegged revenue of Rs. 47, 500 crore for 2015-16 is expected to touch a figure of Rs. 54, 700 crore for 2016-17 at an annual growth rate of 14.7 %. Industry estimates say that advertising sector in India is expected to touch a revenue base of Rs. 99, 400 crore by 2020 at a CAGR of 15.9 % *(FICCI-KPMG: 2016).*

Top 15 advertisers in India account for three-fourth of the business with four companies-*Hindustan Thompson Associates* (HTA), *Mudra Communications Ltd., McCann-Erickson India Ltd, Ogilvy & Mather Ltd.* and *Rediffusion –DY&R-* having a share of 50 percent of the industry outlay *(Kohli: 2005).*

Same is the case with market research agencies, more or less. At present top 7-8 such agencies in the country account for more than three-fourth of the business of market research. Many of these agencies have gone for tie ups and acquisitions with foreign partners leading to a monopolistic trend in this Rs. 1200 crore industry segment. This industry also has an FDI facility of 100 per cent equity *(Rao: 2006; dipp.nic.in/English/policies/FDI_Circular_2015. pdf:2015).*

Table 01

Overall advertising industry size (INR billion)

Segment	2008	2009	2010	2011	2012	2013	2014	2015	Growth in 2015 over 2014	2016p	2017p	2018p	2019p	2020p	CAGR (2015-20P)
TV	82.0	88.0	103.0	116.0	124.8	135.9	154.9	181.3	17.0%	210.3	241.8	275.7	319.8	364.5	15 %
Print	108.0	110.4	126.0	139.4	149.6	162.6	176.4	189.3	7.3%	204	221.7	241.6	263.3	285.8	8.6%
Radio	8.4	8.3	10.0	11.5	12.7	14.6	17.2	19.81	5.3%	23.4	28.4	32.7	37.8	43.3	16.9 %
OOH	16.1	13.7	16.5	17.8	18.2	19.3	22.0	24.41	0.9%	28.3	31.6	35.4	40.0	45.2	13.1%
Digital advertising	6.0	8.0	10.0	15.4	21.7	30.1	43.5	60.13	8.2%	81.1	113.6	153.3	199.3	255.2	33.5 %
Total	221	228	266	300	327	362.5	414.0	475	14.7%	547	637	739	860	994	15.9 %

(Source: FICCI-KPMG report-2016, p—projected)

Ads dictate edits

News today means what sells to the market directly and advertisers indirectly. Market liberalization has made media more of a corporate entity than a community voice. New definitions and new values dictate the news media of today which has been operating in an atmosphere of consumerism *(Raman: 2008, Survey by the author)*.

30 years ago, 55-77% of the total revenue of the newspapers came from readers; today it is the advertisers who sustain the media. From a supplementary component (25-30%) few decades ago to that of supportive component (60-75%) at present, the share of advertising has gone through an upswing all these years. In case of television channels it has been upto 70-80%. This is to the extent of determining priorities and preoccupations in a media outlet. In case of some big media houses, advertising comprises 60% of the total revenues of the group *(Karkaria: 2003, Rao: 2006)*.

That clearly speaks of the pressure or influence advertisers would exert on the content being churned out by the present day media outlets.

A growing regional, language media

There has been a considerable growth and expansion of regional or local media in the country as against the English language press. In the Southern states, Telugu, Kannada and Malyalam dailies have exhibited considerable growth and the same is true about Hindi and northern states.

During 2015-16, while English press grew below 8%, regional newspapers grew in double digits *(FICCI-KPMG: 2016)*.

This is more so because of the localization of the content and setting up of bureaus or district editions as has been successfully done by the Telugu daily *Eenadu (Jeffery: 2001)*.

To ride on positive advertiser sentiment several newspapers have launched local editions in regional languages. For instance, *The Times of India* has entered deep down South in Kerala and Tamil Nad while *The Hindu* has launched its third edition in Kozhikode, besides introducing a printing facility at Mohali in Punjab which has helped the newspaper in good penetration across states of Punjab, Haryan, Himachal Pradesh and J&K *(Consultative Paper, TRAI: 2013).*

Similarly, there are about 7-8 states in the country where monopoly of a single media house is on the rise. It means that more than 50 percent of the viewership, readership and circulation in these states belong to the same group. Likewise in states like Kerala, Gujarat and Rajasthan two dailies have been dominating the media scene, with a significant share in both circulation and readership *(Rao: 2006).*

There are more than 10 media groups in the country emerging as conglomerates in news, entertainment, media distribution and network business. They own newspapers, magazines, radio, television, cable etc. *(Table 02).*

Table 02

Emerging scene of cross media interests in India

Media House	Stakes in...
Sun TV	Newspaper, DTH, Cable, Radio, Magazines, films, telecom
Essel Group (Zee TV)	TV, Cable, Film, Newspaper, radio, DTH, internet
STAR India	TV, film, internet, Newspaper, Cable, DTH
Enadu	Films, TV, Newspaper, Magazines
Living Media (India Today Group)	Radio, TV News, Magazines, Newspaper, internet, events
BCCL(The Times Group)	Radio, TV, internet, Magazines, Newspapers, films, events
Bhaskar	Cable TV, TV, Newspaper
Dainik Jagran	TV News, TV, Radio, Newspapers
Dina Thanti	TV, Radio, Cable TV, Newspapers, Magazines
Mid-Day	Radio, TV, Newspapers

(Source: Country Report, *Mapping Digital Media: India,* Open Society Foundations, New Delhi, 2013; *TRAI: 2013; cmsindia.org/roundtable: 2008)*

No independent media watchdog group

At present there are no active media watch dog groups in India which could be on constant vigil and actively engaged in analysis and research on media issues based on objective analysis and reliable methodology. That is why we often hear about rows over TRP ratings or circulation figures which often are alleged to be subjective *(Raman: 2008)*.

With the choicest TRP ratings or circulation figures on its side, any media outlet can get away with any slot. It becomes a matter of gate keeping only *(Rao: 2006)*.

Though the proposed Broadcast Bill envisages the setting up of an independent Broadcast Regulatory Authority of India (BRAI) with terms of reference to look into the issues of cross media, content, subscription and live sports feed etc., the body is yet to come into force and in what form nobody knows as the Broadcast Bill is yet to be tabled in the parliament *(pib.nic.in/ pressreleases: 2009)*.

Even the TRAI and ASCI, Hyderabad's various reports have stressed the need for setting up of a regulatory body in the country to look into these issues.

Murdoch in India

Rupert Murdoch, the global rule buster and media predator, has already set his foot in India. That is at least what the statistics tell us about. Murdoch and his Star TV are in India now for more than a decade or so. In this period it has risen to the second position (set to become No.1 media house of India) in terms of revenues and reach, after the Bennett Coleman & Company Ltd. At present 70 percent of NewsCorp's Asian revenue comes from Star India alone where it is the top most broadcaster in the country followed by ZEE Telefilms and a distant Prasar Bharti Corporation *(Kumari: 2008, Kohli: 2005)*.

It was this threat that led the local media moghuls including the owners of *The Times of India, India Today, Zee* etc. to come together on one platform which was named Indian Media Group (IMG). IMG tried successfully with the Government of India and got the FDI rules revised to minimise the foreign control of the Indian media and prevent Murdoch from further spreading his influence *(Sridhar: 2003)*.

Currently, Star's cross media Indian operations include entry into newspaper, internet, mobile entertainment, cable, radio and Home video. Interestingly, Star TV India has dropped TV from its name and is rechristened as Star India only *(Chintala: 2008)*.

And despite the caps imposed by the Government, Murdoch already has some key allies in India. It includes Aveek Sarkar of Anand Bazaar Patrika for ABP News, Tata Sons for DTH, Rahejas for cable distribution, Mittals for Radio and Goenkas for film distribution *(Rao: 2006)*.

New media, new style

The opening of Indian media to global giants, immediately after the wave of economic liberalization led to a cultural flow from the outside. Foreign channels brought with them a new westernized style of presentation, cultural mannerism and social etiquettes. Many media professionals consider this new change a welcome thing to follow. But quite others view it as a consumer demand from the audience while another set of public opinion takes it as a sort of cultural aggression.

Slick packaging is the buzz word both in television and even in newspapers now. Almost all big newspapers are in colour, sleek size and pages are designed much more aesthetically than ever before *(Survey conducted by the author, see Chapter Eight for details)*.

Television, the primary source of information

Television has now become the source of instant and primary information by way of its round the clock availability. Frequent news breaks, live- ins and voice- overs have led television channels to surpass newspapers as the primary source of news, particularly political, stock market and sports news. It has led to an 'appetizer effect' among consumers where they search for more of the same or same of the more from various cross media outlets *(Raman: 2008)*.

In 2015, television industry in India grew at 14.2% driven by increased advertising and on account of enhanced marketing budgets of e-commerce companies. Advertising revenue projections for 2016 are Rs.21,030 crore up from Rs.18,130 crore in 2015. During the last year, the television industry showed a healthy growth of 17% in ad spends.

In the coming four years i.e. by 2020, television industry in India is expected to cross a whopping figure of Rs. 1, 09, 760 crore at a CAGR of 15.10 %.

Digitization of the cable sector, although not yet complete, has achieved critical mass. Changes in channel pricing like the introduction of a la carte also made a difference to the structure of the industry. The entertainment television industry also expanded last year with the launch of new channels such as *Zindagi, Sony Pal* and, more recently *&TV (FICCI-KPMG: 2015, 2016)*.

It is here that cross media ownership can have a deciding and critical role in controlling the information flow to the consumers. For example a story carried by a website or news channel when reported ditto by a newspaper from the same group has a much more superimposing effect on the minds of the consumers than something coming out of routine.

Of all these trends however, FDI into country's media industry is an issue in currency with a lot of activity taking place on the media landscape. FDI is also the second biggest thing to happen in the country's media history after the introduction of television in 1970s.

Let us now analyse the scope and extent of Foreign Investment in media in detail.

Foreign investment in Indian media

Post liberalization of 1990s, Indian economy continues to perform strongly and one of the key sectors that benefited from this fast economic growth is the Entertainment & Media (E&M) industry. This is because the industry is a cyclic one that grows faster when the economy is expanding. It also grows faster than the nominal GDP during all phases of economic activity due to its income elasticity wherein when incomes rise, more resources get spent on leisure and entertainment and less on necessities *(FICCI-KPMG Reports: 2014, 2015, 2016)*.

Further, consumption spending itself is increasing due to rising disposable incomes on account of sustained growth in income levels, and this also builds the case for a strong bullish growth in the sector.

The Media & Entertainment industry in the country estimated at Rs. 1,15,700 crore for 2015-16 as against Rs. 58, 000 crore in 2007 is expected to register a Compounded Annual Growth Rate (CAGR) of 14.3 per cent to touch Rs 2,26, 000 crore by 2020 wherein digital advertising has emerged to have the highest growth rate of 38.2 per cent during the last year while all other sub-sectors are expected to grow at a CAGR in the range of 7-34 per cent*(ibid.)*.

Curiously, the FDI inflow in the media sector from April 2000 to Feb 2015 has been to the tune of Rs 19,197.30 crore *(dipp.nic.in/English/Publications/ FDI_Statistics:2015)*.

Here is brief sketch of the growth pattern of Indian media industry:

Table 03

Industry size and projections

Overall industry Size (Rs billion)	2008	2009	2010	2011	2012	2013	2014	2015	Growth in 2015 over 2014	2016p	2017p	2018p	2019p	CAGR (2014-19p)
TV	241	257	297	329	370.1	417.2	474.9	542.2	14.2%	617.0	709.6	823.3	956.8	1097.6	15.10%
Print	172	175.2	192.9	208.8	224.1	243.1	263.4	283.4	7.6%	305.2	329.6	355.9	383.6	412.5	7.8 %
Films	104	89.3	83.3	92.9	112.4	125.3	126.4	138.2	9.3%	158.7	174.1	190.0	207.8	227.3	10.5%
Radio	8.4	8.3	10	11.5	12.7	14.6	17.2	19.8	15.3%	23.4	28.4	32.7	37.8	43.3	16.9 %
Music	7.4	7.8	8.6	9.0	10.6	9.6	9.8	10.8	10.2%	12.1	14.0	16.1	18.4	20.6	13.8%
OOH	16.1	13.7	16.5	17.8	18.2	19.3	22.0	24.4	10.9%	28.3	31.6	35.4	40.0	45.2	13.9%
Animation and VFX	17.5	20.1	23.7	31.0	35.3	39.7	44.9	51.1	13.8%	58.3	67.1	78.1	91.3	108.0	16.1%
Gaming	7.0	8.0	10	13.0	15.3	19.2	23.5	26.5	12.8%	30.8	34.4	39.0	45.4	50.7	13.9%
Digital Advt.	6.0	8.0	10	15.4	21.7	30.1	43.5	60.1	38.2%	81.1	113.6	153.3	199.3	255.2	33.5%
Total	**580**	**587**	**652**	**728**	**821**	**918**	**1026**	**1157**	**12.8%**	**1315**	**1502**	**1724**	**1980**	**2260**	**14.3%**

(Source: FICCI-KPMG report-2016, p—projected)

FDI, how and what

The debate over foreign investment in media in India is as old as the country's independent existence. The subject was discussed in the First Press Commission under the title of "foreign nationals as owners" and the report viewed it with "disfavour"*(First Press Commission: 1954)*.

In 1955 the Union Cabinet endorsed this view and decided against any foreign investment in the press. The Second Press Commission also discussed the subject in the context of "foreign money in the Indian press" and recommended "there should be a specific legal provision under which no newspaper undertaking should have any foreign ownership either in the form of shares or in the form of loans"*(Second Press Commission: 1982, Noorani: 2008)*.

However, things have changed considerably since then. The country has shifted from a socialistic mode of economy to a liberal economy. The Government has opened up many sectors including core sectors like oil exploration, nuclear energy, deep-sea mining etc. for foreign investment and the country is witnessing massive investment from foreign players*(ficci.com/media-room.asp:2008)*.

Media in India has grown up considerably in the last about two decades of economic liberalization. Media has been gradually opened up for foreign investment with encouraging results as is evident from various industry reports and surveys from time to time.

The Indian Media industry has significantly benefited from the liberal foreign direct investment (FDI) regime and most segments of the E&M industry today allow foreign investment. Now the FDI is even permitted in the two core sectors of the industry as well-print media and radio. Films, advertising, television and other segments are already open to foreign investment to the extent of 100 percent FDI through the automatic route *(FICCI-KPMG Reports: 2014, 2015, 2016)*.

Printing of facsimile editions of foreign journals is now also allowed in India. This policy is helping foreign journals save on the cost of distribution while servicing the Indian audiences more effectively *(Circular-I&B Ministry, 2006; dipp.nic.in/English/policies/FDI_Circular_2015.pdf:2015)*.

The FM radio sector too is now open for foreign investment with 26 percent FDI being allowed. There are over 250 FM (frequency modulation) radio stations in the country (and the number is likely to cross 1,200 in five years). As a result, radio sector is expanding rapidly with forecast growth rate of 16.9 percent per annum to capture an expected market of Rs. 4330 crore by 2020 *(FICCI-KPGM: 2016)*.

However, all this goes with its own set of guidelines. As a consequence, media industry has witnessed increasing fund flows in most of its segments, including print media. Examples include foreign investment in English press such as *Hindustan Times, Business Standard* and *India Today* by Henderson Global, Financial Times and Daily Mail respectively. Vernacular media too got its share of foreign investment with a strategic equity investment by Independent News & Media in *Dainik Jagran*, a leading Hindi newspaper.

In the broadcasting sphere, most channels beaming into India (such as Walt Disney, ESPN-Star Sports, Star, Discovery, BBC etc.) established foreign investment subsidiary companies for content development and advertisement of airtime sales *(FICCI-PwC: 2006, FICCI-KPMG: 2014)*.

In the television distribution space arena, foreign investment is being drawn by the larger cable operators referred to as 'multi-system operators (MSO)' such as Hathway and Hindujas. Similarly, in the television content space, the investment in Nimbus Communications by a foreign private equity player is just another example of foreign investment inflow.

Infact, the titles cleared for FDI includes proposals from brands like *Mid-Day Multimedia Ltd, Business India Publications Ltd, Deccan Chronicle Holdings Ltd, Dhara Prakashan Pvt. Ltd, Writers & Publishers Ltd* and *DT Media & Entertainment Pvt. Ltd. (pib.nic.in/pressreleases: 2009, Swarup: 2007)*.

Filmfare getting FDI for its products like *Filmfare Classics, Filmfare Star Beauty* and *Filmfare Star Homes* from Worldwide Media Ltd., Infomedia India Ltd and IDG Media Pvt. Ltd. having diluted their stake in Cricinfo Magazine and Indian Channel World are a few other such cases *(Report, Business Standard: June 22, 2006)*.

Over the last fifteen years, the Entertainment and Media industry has attracted FDI inflow to the tune of Rs 19,197.30 crore from April 2000 to Feb 2015 *(dipp.nic.in/English/Publications/FDI_Statistics:2015)*.

Some of the larger FDI investments have been in HT Media Ltd, which sold off 24.64 per cent stakes for Rs 193.99 crores, and *Jagaran Prakashan* that offloaded 26 per cent equity for Rs 3.21 crores. *Business Standard* too sold 13.85 per cent shares to Financial Times for Rs 8.37 crores *(Report, Business Standard: June 22, 2006.)*

The growth of Indian Media & Entertainment industry has been phenomenal and FDI has been a significant contributor in this.

Table 04

Select illustrations of strategic foreign investments in the Indian E&M industry

Foreign investor	Indian entity	Segment	Nature of investment	Reason
Virgin Radio Asia	HT Media	FM radio	Equity stake	Entry into FM radio segment
Financial Times (Pearson Group)	Business Standard	Newspaper publishing-print media	Equity stake	Expansion and strengthening of operations
Independent News & Media, UK	Jagran Prakashan	Newspaper publishing-print media	Equity stake	Expansion and strengthening of operations
T Rowe Price International	Mid-Day Multimedia	Newspaper publishing-print media	Equity stake	Expansion and strengthening of operations
AMP Hendersen, UK	HT Media	Newspaper publishing-print media	Equity stake	Expansion and strengthening of operations
Bear Stearns	Adlab Films	Film production & exhibition	Equity stake	Expansion of operations
3i(UK based private equity FTSE 100) company	Nimbus Communications	Television & films	Equity stake	Expansion and strengthening of operations

Americorp ventures, Mauritius based	Nimbus Communications	Television & films	Equity stake	Expansion and strengthening of operations
Americorp ventures, Mauritius based	Asianet Communications	Television broadcasting	Equity stake	Expansion and strengthening of operations
Dubai based NRI group	Yantra Media	Television content provider in South India	Equity stake	Expansion and strengthening of operations in South India and entry into Hindi television content market
New Vernon Bharat, Mauritius based	Jagran TV	Television production & broadcasting	Equity stake	Expansion and strengthening of operations
Reuters, UK	Times Global Broadcasting	Television production & broadcasting	Equity stake	Expansion and strengthening of operations

(Source: FICCI-PwC Report: 2006)

Dissenting voices too

But despite all this optimism, there are still voices in the media industry who want easing of the equity caps or waiving off any other limits for foreign investors intending to invest in media industry in India.

Dileep Padgaonkar, Chairman, Asia Pacific Communication Associates, New Delhi, thinks the 26 % equity on FDI in news media is very little and argues when the Government allowed cent per cent FDI in Atomic Energy, what was the logic of putting a ceiling in media which, arguably, won't encourage the big investors to put in money in India under the current limits. On the argument that lower equity helps Indian entities or audience insolate from influences or dictates of outside media owners and control lies with Indian owners even in outlets where investment has been made, Padgaonkar cites the example of STAR television which, in an effort to become the highest revenue earning television company, has almost Indianised its domestic content with *Saas-Bahu, Kasuti* and other serials becoming a household name and an average viewer identifying himself or herself with its content. After all a media company is in business to make profit that it cannot do by alienating or offending the local audience and the host country's tastes and likings, he argues*(Padgaonkar: 2007)*.

This argument is also shared by Payal Kohli, editor, *Cosmopolitan*, who believes that the purpose of allowing FDI in media would be defeated through its own executors if the equity caps are not further relaxed to allow many big investors to invest in Indian media industry *(Kohli: 2006)*.

Cosmopolitan, an India Today Group publication is in a content partnership with a US Group, Hearst Corporation. About 20% of Cosmo content comes from it, rest 80% is generated locally.

If the FDI norms are relaxed more and more such publishing concerns of international repute would come to India, they contend.

But definitely, foreign investment has rejuvenated the media landscape in India. Many brands like The Times, Living Media etc., as we will see in the following chapter, have gone in for new ventures with the help of FDI to write and consolidate their success stories. Other media giants also, taking full advantage of a booming economy, have established themselves as big players on the media turf of the country.

CHAPTER – SIX

India's Media Barons

Indian media is expanding like never before. The Indian Entertainment and Media industry grew by 12.8 % during last year and in the coming four year years i.e. by 2020 the industry size is expected to be Rs. 2,26,000 crore at an estimated CAGR of 14.30% *(FICCI-KPMG Report: 2016)*.

Moreover, with the facilitation of Foreign Direct Investment and tie-ups with international news organizations things have become much easier for the media conglomerates to expand their activities and operations beyond their parent streams of activity.

In India, there are media houses whose interests extend beyond just one realm of activity. Living Media India Ltd., of the *India Today* and *Aaj Tak* fame, Bennett Coleman & Co. (BCCL), owners of *The Times of India*, *The Economic Times*, *Femina*, *Filmfare*, *Times NOW* and *Zoom TV*, etc. are just two names among the lot.

The India Today Group publishes, apart from its weekly flagship publication-*India Today*, daily newspaper, *Mail Today*, magazines like *India Today International*, *Cosmopolitan*, *Business Today*, *Computers Today*, *India Today Plus*, *India Today International* and other magazines and journals. And of course, one each news channel in Hindi (*AajTak*) and English (*Headlines Today*).

Similarly, Times Group or BCCL comes up with its brand publication; *The Times of India* from multiple cities across India. The Group has other notable brands like *The Economic Times, Navbharat Times, Filmfare, Femina, Maharashtra Times, Radio Mirchi, Planet M* and portal site *indiatimes.com* in its kitty. The company is also into electronic newsgathering with a 24-hour English news channel, *Times NOW* and a very successful lifestyle channel, *Zoom TV (www.indiatimes.com/aboutus.cms, 2008)*.

Media companies like NDTV and Zee TV and some new entries to the field are also expanding their activities beyond their areas of core competence.

However, it needs a deeper look to know about these media groups, their ascendancy and realms of activity to understand the basic question of cross media ownership in India.

BENNETT COLEMAN & CO. LTD. (*Times Group*)

The first edition of The Bombay Times and Journal of Commerce, later to be called *The Times of India*, was launched in Bombay (Now Mumbai) in 1838. After several years of change, evolution and growth in the paper's character Bennett Coleman & Co. Ltd, the proprietors of *The Times of India*, was established with the principal objective of publishing newspapers, journals, magazines and books. Today, Bennett Coleman & Co. Ltd (BCCL) is India's largest media house with about Rs. 1600 crores as annual turnover *(Kohli: 2010)*.

The growth and reach of Times Group in the last two decades has been spectacular and interesting to observe. From Rs. 4.70 crore as profit in 1987-88, BCCL's profits jumped to a whopping Rs. 130 crore on the revenues of Rs. 479 crore in the 12 months ending July, 1994. Today BCCL is India's largest media company in terms of revenues *(Padgaonkar: 2007)*.

The real shift, analysts say, came in mid 80s when Samir Jain took over the mantle of BCCL in 1986. The changeover was imperative as all other businesses of the Jain family---New Central Jute and Rohtas Industries were in decline-the Jain family owns the BCCL *(Kohli: 2010)*.

Jain looked at the newspaper as any other brand or product and employed all available marketing strategies to promote his "product". From colour supplements to different pricing on different days to advertisement encroachments into editorial space, he did everything to maximise the returns. This strategy yielded excellent results and led to the shutting down of some rival publications then including the much talked about *Illustrated weekly of India* etc. as they could not sustain the competition thrown by Jain.

Subsequently Times Group overtook *Hindustan Times,* the market leader in Delhi then and today with a claimed circulation of 2.14 million copies *The Times* is now country's only truly national newspaper. An estimated 60-70% of BCCL revenue comes from its Mumbai edition only. BCCL also claims it to be world's largest selling English broadsheet daily, ahead even of *USA Today (Padgaonkar: 2007).*

At present The Times Group is a multi-edition, multi-product, multi-media organisation, and has to its credit several leading publications. These include *The Times of India, The Economic Times, Navbharat Times, Maharashtra Times, Femina* and *Filmfare* etc.

The Group also has interests in other sectors of media industry in the form of Radio Mirchi, *Planet M,* Times Music and Times Multimedia. In April 2000, Times Internet Ltd, a wholly owned subsidiary of Bennett Coleman & Co. Ltd, was floated to handle the Group's Internet properties.

The Group has also a significant and dominant presence in electronic media as well. *Zoom TV* is India's first non-fiction, Hindi entertainment channel that it claims to be a source for celebrities, Bollywood, spicy gossip, unabashed glamour and the high life. The Group also owns *Times NOW,* a 24-hour urbane packaged news channel. It is a joint venture of BCCL and Reuters Ltd. London and reportedly doing well. In 2009 it also launched ET NOW, a financial news channel in collaboration with Reuters London *(indiatimes.com/aboutus.cms:2006, Open Society Foundations: 2013).*

On June 15, 2006 BCCL signed an agreement to acquire 100% stakes in Bangalore based Vijayanand Printers Ltd. (VPL) –which published two Kanada newspapers, *Vijay Karnataka* and *Usha Kiran* and the English daily *Vijay Times.* All these three newspapers have ten editions *(PCI, Annual Report: 2007).*

Deepening its hold further in South, The Times Group also launched its Chennai edition on April 14, 2008 and Goa edition on May 06, 2008 *(Karkaria: 2003)*.

In this whole process, however, BCCL and Jain in particular were criticized for starting price war in the newspaper industry. Jain was also accused of eroding circulation revenues and importantly encroaching editorial space by advertisements. But despite this re invented BCCL became a role model and Jain an icon for many in the media to follow later on. But in all what Jain brought was not an improvement in his company's efficiency alone but a change of mindset where newspaper was now thought of as a product, generating revenue.

The changes Samir Jain brought to *The Times* later proved to be a precursor to the economic liberalization in India. Subsequently newsprint and printing machinery in India were brought under Open General License category and multinational advertising agencies started coming to India.

BCCL is a glaring example where the consequences of cross media ownership are much more pronounced and explicit. A news story reported by Times NOW or Zoom TV on one day, is carried by *The Times of India* which in turn pushes it across all segments. Similarly, the Femina Miss India Contest gets both pre and post event publicity in all the outlets of BCCL, thus raising the sales for the company. It decimates the cross-sectoral limits and creates the impact of one medium on another. It also shows that with infrastructure and technology available they can blow something out of proportion and black out some other. The only question is; when and if it suits them. The situation results in influencing public opinion on a particular line and the audiences are prevented from getting diversity of version.

BCCL is also in a tie up with foreign investors under several FDI regimes. Apart from its news channels, which have 26% stakes from Reuters, its brands like Filmfare and Femina would be getting FDI for products like *Filmfare Classics, Filmfare Star Beauty* and *Filmfare Star Homes* from Worldwide Media Ltd *(Swarup: 2007)*.

Already brands like *Filmfare* and Femina Miss India contest etc are, as cases of brand extension, money-spinners for the BCCL *(Kohli: 2010)*.

The Group has envisioned as a high-quality research university in the National Capital Region of India offering undergraduate, graduate and doctoral degrees in engineering and technology, management and entrepreneurship, law, design, media and liberal arts, and applied sciences.

Bennett University, as it has been named, recently entered into an academic collaboration with Babson Global Consortium for Entrepreneurship Educators for imparting world class education *(economictimes.indiatimes.com:2015)*.

Zee Television Network

What can be described as India's first privately owned Hindi satellite television channel, Zee Telefilms Limited was founded in October 1992 as a part of Asia Today Ltd., on a 50:50 joint venture basis between STAR and Zee. Promoted by Subhash Chandra, one of India's leading entrepreneurs, it began with three-hour largely film based programming broadcasts before graduating to sitcoms and soaps.

When Rupert Murdoch's News Corp Limited acquired the satellite distribution business of STAR, News Corp de facto became a partner of Zee *(Kohli: 2010)*.

Zee's launch gave the Indian audience what it had been waiting for and subsequently the market took off. Cable penetration increased and the business thrived. From about 4,500 homes being cabled daily in the first half of 1992, the number more than doubled to 9,450 homes daily in the second half *(Kohli:2003)*.

To further develop the relationship, News Corp and Zee subsequently co-founded Siticable, one of the leading cable MSOs in India.

In March 2000, after a six-year joint venture, Zee bought News Corp's stake in both the broadcasting business and Siticable *(Raman: 2008)*.

Zee News has been a pioneer and a leader in the field of investigative journalism, with programming that goes deeper and far beyond the usual news and current affairs programmes. Programs like *The Inside Story* have brought Zee a distinct style. *News Top 10, Prime Time Special, Bollywood Baazigar, Bole Toh Bollywood* etc. are the segments which have given the channel a place of distinction *(ibid.)*.

Presently the basket of Zee comprises 15 channels. It includes a general entertainment channel (Zee TV as it is called), a movie channel (Zee Cinema), a news channel (Zee News), a channel for English films (Zee MGM), an

English entertainment channel (Zee English), and five regional language channels. It has a good overseas market in UK and US. Old hits like *Amaanat* and *Parivartan* were huge success with Asian community in UK in 2000 *(Kohli: 2005).*

Its overseas audience network stretches out to more than 60 countries in the world.

Since it was an experiment first of its kind in private television in India, Zee brought with it a new stylebook of fashion and lifestyle to which the viewers in India were not yet exposed. Many channels later joined this bandwagon and reinforced this trend. These trends gradually got assimilated and accepted in the societal routine of the country. These trends later gave the fashion, cosmetic and image making industries a big kick in the country *(Kohli: 2010).*

LIVING MEDIA INDIA LTD *(India Today Group)*

When the chartered accountant Aroon Poorie ventured into publishing in mid-70s, no body, including himself, could have imagined that one day he would be the trailblazer of media industry in India.

India Today, a serious fortnightly newsmagazine aimed at Indians living out of the country, was published with a modest print order of 5,000 copies in December 1975. Today Living Media India is a multi sectoral media group with stakes and interest in television, book publishing, music, printing, events, radio etc. In print it publishes, in addition to now-weekly *India Today*, which is the flagship media outlet of the Living Media India Limited, 15 other magazines on varied subjects of life like finance, health, housekeeping, lifestyle, business etc. *(Raman: 2008).*

In 2008 it came up with a daily tabloid newspaper, *Mail Today*, in a joint venture with Associated Newspapers, London, publishers of *Daily Mail.* Already the Group has foreign collaboration in publishing one of its other prominent splits, *Cosmopolitan. Cosmopolitan*, catering to the niche modern workingwoman in metropolitan India, was launched in 1996 under licence from Hearst Corporation, USA.

The Group is also into the marketing of *Readers Digest* and *Time* magazine *(Kohli: 2006, guardian.co.uk/media:2008).*

The India Today Conclave has emerged recently as a big interactive media event where policy makers, politicians, leaders and activists across the globe share a common platform and vision with a select gathering. The event gets a good media support from its sister outlets in print, radio, internet and television (*http://conclave.digitaltoday.in/conclave2008*).

Thus substantiating the case for cross media limits. The Group has all along advocated for relaxing foreign investment norms in media industry in India.

Further diversifying its investment portfolio, on May 18, 2012, India's leading business house-Aditya Birla Group-announced to pick a 27.5% stake in Living Media India with its chairman, Aroon Purie describing it as a means to aggressively address the future potential of Indian media business *(Report, livemint: May 12, 2012)*.

India Today Group's foray into the electronic medium dates back to pre-liberalised times of 1980s with the incorporation of TV Today Network (TVTN) in 1988 and the launch of much famed video newsmagazine, *Newstrack*. VHS copies of the electronic newsmagazine used to be sold through video parlours and during the 90s' Kashmir violence and following Mandal agitation, *Newstrack* recorded an all time high television viewership. Subsequently, however, it lost its tempo and it had to be stopped *(indiatoday. digitaltoday.in: 2008)*.

In its renewed effort, TV Today Network launched Hindi news and current affairs programme, *AajTak*, in 1995 on the Metro channel of Doordarshan. Soon the programme became increasingly popular for its style and comprehensive coverage of the news.

Later, the Group launched a 24-hour Hindi news & current affairs channel by the same name—*AajTak* on December 31, 2000.

From a 25-minute news capsule on the terrestrial network, TV Today Network, India's one of the large news networks today, consists of four news channels– *AajTak, Headlines Today, Tez* and *Dilli Aaj Tak*. Having got all its channels now encrypted, TV Today Network intends to make its forays in international markets. Already *Aaj Tak* and *Headlines Today* are available in the US on the Echostar platform, via the Dish Network. The Group claims its channels' popularity in the US has been increasing exponentially ever since their launch in October 2005 there *(ibid.)*.

At present TV Today Network Ltd. is a listed company on the stock exchanges and LMI has 57.11 % stakes in it *(livemint.com: 2012)*.

Capitalising on Delhi's rising consumerism, booming economy and rapidly improving infrastructure, the Group has also branched off part of its metro content into a full fledged channel called *Dilli Aaj Tak*. The success of *Dilli Aaj Tak* forced its arch rival-NDTV to launch its own version on urban life— *MetroNation*, though on a much sophisticated scale. *Tez- Khbrain Phataphat* as they call it, a news capsule based channel with shorter news wheels and no long winded discussions or analyses, has been the other product of the umbrella group.

The Group also has the credit to launch country's first ever women's radio station, *Meow* 104.8 FM *(delhi.meowfm.com/index.php?option=com_content&t ask=view&id=12&Itemid=27: 2008)*.

India Today Group also qualifies as a good case to study the cross media ownership issue and its related consequences. In 1997, for example, it ran a story based on the leaks from the special investigation team probing the assassination of former Prime Minister Rajiv Gandhi. The impact and reach was so much that it led to the fall of the then United Front Government.

Moreover, the Group has been advocating, in its own way, for relaxing the rules for entry of foreign media into the country and other regulations which suit the Group from time to time.

New Delhi Television Ltd. (NDTV)

What started with a half-an-hour current affairs programme on world politics in late 80s on Doordarshan has grown up to a bouquet of six satellite channels in India.

Owned and promoted by veteran sephologist and analyst Dr. Prannoy Roy and his journalist wife Radhika Roy, New Delhi Television Limited (NDTV Ltd.) has a future vision of launching about fifty channels, many of them outside India in countries like Malaysia, Europe and Africa etc. *(ndtv.com/ convergence/ndtv/corporatepage/index.aspx:2008)*.

In 1998 NDTV joined STAR News for content sharing which had recently started beaming its signals to India but was unable to start its own news operations due to legal hitches. The agreement lasted till March 2003 when the two partners parted ways. On April 14, 2003, NDTV Ltd. evolved into an independent news broadcaster by simultaneously launching two news channels, *NDTV 24X7* in English and *NDTV India* in Hindi. The company also launched a 24-hour business channel, *NDTV Profit* on January 17, 2005. In 2008 it added two more channels to its bouquet. *NDTV Imagine* deals exclusively with soft entertainment like soaps while *NDTV Metro* and *NDTV Good Times* are up-market lifestyle channels dedicated to global urban Indian and issues confronting the present day metro society *(Dutt: 2007)*.

On June 13, 2006 it launched the 'Southern Edition'- a daily news programme using the Opt-Out telecast technology–for its viewers in Tamil Nadu, Karnataka and Kerala. With the latest technology, a first in India, it will be possible for the viewers to see news specific to their region even as the national telecast continues *(Raman: 2008)*.

NDTV has also launched its first channel outside India in partnership with Astro, a leading South East Asia media group. *Astro Awani*, launched in Malaysia, is a 24 hour news, infotainment and lifestyle channel. It also used its expertise to launch a global channel-Independent Television-with Beximco Group in Bangladesh.

Over the years, NDTV has expanded its brand portfolio to seize opportunities in the 'beyond news space' and has step-down subsidiaries: NDTV Lifestyle, NDTV Convergence and NDTV Worldwide offering high end consultancy for setting up of local television news channels in emerging markets across the world *(ndtv.com:2008)*.

The company has a network of 20 news bureaus in the country and abroad like Pakistan, UK and USA etc, all of which are connected live to the main office in New Delhi. It was the first news company to use VSNL's V-SAT satellite communication terminals for newsgathering. It also had plans to use helicopters for newsgathering but was not allowed by the aviation authorities due to security restrictions *(Kohli: 2005, Dutt: 2007)*.

Posting a consolidated income of Rs.586 crore and post tax profits of Rs.46 crores for the year ending March 31, 2015, the company has registered a growth of 19% over the last year i.e. year ending March 2014. The Delhi-based company has focused on 'triple play' of synergies between TV, Internet and the mobile phone, a model that's gradually becoming an industry standard across the world *(ndtv.com/convergence/ndtv/corporatepage/annual_report.aspx:2015)*.

Often credited with being the first English news channel to the extent of getting clichéd as the BBC of India, NDTV has certainly brought new insights to broadcast journalism in India. However, with all its infrastructure and network available, NDTV has also become an interesting case to study the cross media ownership subject. For, the same system is used to re-transmit a story from one channel to another or, say, from Hindi speaking viewers to English speaking, from north to South India and so on.

Reliance Industries Ltd.

2014 saw the biggest take over so far in Indian media industry. Has the Rupert Murdoch of India arrived?, media critics of the country are keeping their fingers crossed.

A striking example of ownership concentration in media, Reliance Industries Limited (RIL) in 2014 took control of ownership of one of the country's largest regional language news enterprises-ETV, Network18 and its subsidiary TV18, the listed entity which controls channels such as CNBC-TV18, CNBC Awaaz, CNN-IBN, IBN7, IBN-Lokmat, websites (*firstpost.com*, *moneycontrol.com*), magazines (including the license for Forbes India), entertainment channel (*Colors, MTV and Homeshop Entertainment*) among other businesses, through an Independent Media Trust (IMT) *(Mehta: 2015)*.

RIL for its own part declared that this 'acquisition will differentiate Reliance's 4G business by providing a unique amalgamation at the intersect of telecom, web and digital commerce via a suite of premier digital properties'*(livemint: 2014)*.

It was a set of complex financial nitty gritties, though permissible under law, that finally sealed the deal. But nevertheless it raised questions.

It was actually in 2008 that Reliance, considered as India's biggest corporate entity, entered the news market in the country by investing in Eenadu, India's largest regional newsgathering network, quietly. This, however, came to fore in 2011 by chance. It so happened that the wife of former Andhra Pradesh chief minister Y S R Reddy filed a case of disproportionate assets against Telugu Desam Party chief and another former chief minister N, Chandrababu Naidu in the state High Court in October 2011 and sought probe.

One of the allegations she made was that a long time Naidu backer and supporter, Ramoji Rao-founder of Eenadu group-was bailed out by Mukesh Ambani by investing Rs. 2,600 crore in Eenadu when he (Rao) had run into financial crunch.

Subsequently, by mid-2014, Reliance took full management control of Network18 by converting its optional debentures into equity shares.

According to RIL it already controlled various assets in Eenadu's TV empire (100 per cent in the regional news channels ETV Uttar Pradesh, ETV Madhya Pradesh, ETV Rajasthan, ETV Bihar and ETV Urdu channels; 100 per cent in the entertainment channels ETV Marathi, ETV Kannada, ETV Bangla, ETV Gujarati and ETV Oriya and 49 per cent in ETV Telugu and ETV Telugu News). In effect, Reliance then transferred a large part of these shares to Network18/TV18, whose promoters received funding from the Reliance-owned IMT to acquire them through two separate rights issue of shares *(Forbes: 2014)*.

Presently Reliance media empire comprises 13 news channels, 22 entertainment channels, 18 websites, in 11 languages.

In 2012, RIL — through IMT — pumped around Rs 2,200 crore into six holding firms promoted by *Network18*.

The RIL-Network 18-Eenadu Multimedia Empire

13 news channels, 22 entertainment channels, 18 websites, in 11 languages

- CNBC-TV18, CNBC Awaaz, CNBC-Bajar (Gujarati biz channel)
- Flagship business channel CNBC-TV18 enjoys a 56 per cent viewership in the biz channel market
- CNN-IBN, IBN7 and IBN-Lokmat (a Marathi regional news channel in partnership with the Lokmat group), IBN-Gujarati.
- Flagship English news channel CNN-IBN has a relative market share of 27.5 per cent.
- Flagship Hindi news channel IBN7 has 14 per cent of the Hindi news market share
- Colors, Colors HD, MTV, Comedy Central, VH1, Nick, Sonic, Nick Jr./Teen Nick, History TV-18
- moneycontrol.com, Web 18, Newswire 18, HomeShop 18, Bookmyshow.com, IBNlive.com, Firstpost.com
- Network 18 clutch of websites are among the top eight web properties in India with 18.54 million monthly unique visitors
- HomeShop18.com is among the top 6 retail websites with 8.1 million monthly unique visitors
- Magazines: *Forbes India, Overdrive, Better Photography*
- Network of 12 channels, a daily, four magazines, Margadarsi Chits Ltd, Dolphin Group of Hotels, Ramoji Film City
- Eenadu is in the top six among language dailies of the country
- Has four Hindi channels in Madhya Pradesh, Uttar Pradesh, Bihar and Rajasthan
- Entertainment channels in Telugu, Kannada, Bangla, Oriya, Marathi, Urdu and Gujarati
- 24-hour news channels in Telugu and Kannada, Rajasthan, Chhattisgarh, Uttarakhand and Jharkhand
- Most channels occupy No. 3 and No. 4 positions in the viewership ratings in the languages mentioned.

Media analysts believe that such huge investments were made by Reliance to secure preferential access to Network18 and TV18's content for its own 4G broadband services.

On 29 May 2014, RIL took over full management control, with its board approving funding of Rs 4,000 crore to Independent Media Trust, of which RIL is the sole beneficiary, for acquisition of control of Network18 Media and Investments Ltd, including its subsidiary TV18 Broadcast Ltd. RIL reported that the funds would give it 78 per cent control over Network18 Media and 9 per cent in TV18 and also allow it to acquire shares tendered in open offers *(Mehta: 2015)*.

This takeover, once combined with RIL's telecom business, makes the combined group likely bigger than media baron Rupert Murdoch's empire in India and bigger than any other media group in India. And that should raise some serious questions about it.

CHAPTER – SEVEN

Cross Media Ownership: A Survey

After discussing different perspectives of the industry status and the current situation on the subject of cross media ownership, it is important to get a quantitative assessment of it, particularly from the people handling the issues on an almost daily basis.

To get an empirical view of the ownership pattern of Indian media, a field survey was conducted in the form of questionnaires with respondents from all across the country. This was in addition to a series of interviews I had conducted on the subject with a battery of media practitioners and opinion leaders in the media stream across the country.

The survey was aimed at media practitioners, positioned at various levels, who are faced with the question of media ownership and its impact on an almost day-to-day basis. The respondents included reporters, sub editors on the down line and Editors, Managing Editors, Associate Editors and other senior media practitioners on the up line of the hierarchy. All these respondents represented a cross section of the media domain of the country.

Accordingly, two types of questionnaires were framed (See appendix-II & III) depending upon the positions at which the respondents were placed viz a viz the subject and the consequent access they had over the issues related to it. Written questionnaires were preferred over other modes of interaction to get authentic, accurate and well thought out responses based on analytical comprehension rather than opinion or guesswork. It was a self-administered study with respondents getting ample time (from few weeks to a couple of months) to come up with their responses.

The questions were framed keeping in view the knowledge of the subject by the respondents so that they would comprehend these and respond accordingly. Two sets were prepared to get maximum information and experience-based opinion on varied aspects of cross media ownership, depending on their role in decision making and the problems encountered while executing the things on day to day basis.

The questions posed included changing content of the television channels and newspapers and whether the foreign channels have brought with them a new stylebook of fashion and lifestyle. Whether they liked media being concentrated into a few hands only or preferred a much more diffused ownership pattern was another question posed to the respondents. And to ensure the media plurality the respondents were asked to give their suggestions. The respondents were also asked if they agreed with Government making such laws to ensure such a plurality.

The respondents were asked if they agreed that media was going through a phase of Murdochisation (mergers, tie ups, acquisitions etc.). Also, what did they think of cross- media curbs (do these curbs limit their freedom?) and were they in favour of the curbs if put by the Government. They were also asked if they supported a level playing field for small newspapers in order to maintain parity with multi edition large newspaper groups to ensure diversity and plurality of views. In this regard, they were asked what they thought of the Foreign Direct Investment (would it be helpful or discourage media plurality in the country?).

Methodology

The methodology adopted for the survey was based on the principle of sampling keeping in view the vast and diverse fields of media available to the public. The respondents were drawn from as diverse streams like newspapers, magazines, television, public relations, web journalism and other areas. Deliberate attempt was made to include representatives from almost every geographical area and sector of the industry.

Consequently, 120 respondents were chosen and among them 34 were among the top slot of Editors, Managing Editors, Associate Editors and other senior media practitioners like Producers, etc. Among the other 86 respondents, 38 were principal correspondents, special correspondents and chief sub editors. The remaining 48 comprised 36 senior reporters, reporters and anchors, 12 freelance media persons and all others on the down line of the hierarchy *(Table No. 05)*.

Table 05
Designation-wise distribution of the respondents

Designation of respondents	Number
Editors	07
Managing/Executive Editors	10
News Producers/Associate Editors	17
Chief Copy Desk	24
Spl. /Prpl Correspondents	14
Senior Reporters	21
Reporters/Anchors	15
Freelancers	12
Total	**120**

Looking at the streams the respondents came from, 46 belonged to newspapers and magazines. 23 respondents came from television background while as 12 belonged to the PR stream. 32 respondents comprised freelancers and other groups of media practitioners *(Table No. 06).*

Table 06
Stream-wise break up of respondents

Stream	No. of respondents
Newspapers	37
Magazines	09
PR	12
Web journalists	07
Television journalists	23
Others/Freelancers	32
Total	**120**

Gender wise, it was good mix of male and female respondents. Of the 120 respondents, 86 were male media practitioners while the rest (34) were females *(Table No. 07).*

Table 07
Gender wise distribution of respondents to the survey

Gender	No. of respondents
Men	86
Women	34
Total	**120**

Age-wise it was a beautiful blend of experienced and the young talent and all those who responded had their own set of experiences of the consequences of cross media ownership to share.

Area wise also, the respondents came from all across the country like Manipur, Delhi, Kashmir and South India (thus giving the survey a holistic, pan-Indian appeal). Open-ended questions were framed to get more qualitative responses and analyses.

Results of the Survey

Interesting results were thrown up by the survey. For example, all respondents, without an exception, believed that media plurality is good for a vibrant society. "Yes, the ideology of those few people (once media ownership is concentrated into few hands only) is obvious in anything written, spoken or aired", commented R7 (New Delhi). R7's comments reflected a general consensus of respondents on the subject.

The first question asked was whether the respondents agreed that television content was becoming softer to which the respondents had a varied set of explanations to offer. "Sometimes certain channels do go overboard but these days news comes with analysis", says R3 (New Delhi). Similarly, R6 (also New Delhi) though agreeing but attributed it to the changing tastes of public. "Even the news has gone through a change. It is more of gossip, fashion, high profile weddings etc," says R6 (Jammu).

About things like style, food, fashion making it to the front pages of leading print brands like *Hindustan Times* and *The Times of India*, the respondents had a variety of reasons to offer. For R3 (Chandigrah) "it is a case of slick packaging" while N2 (Srinagar) considers it "a sheer case of consumerism meant to earn money". "There is nothing like news today, all columns are sold at a price tag", opines C1 (Hyderabad). 84 respondents (70%) share the feeling that soft stuff like celebrity news and lifestyle dominate the front pages for which R4 (Bangalore) asks these media units "to do a serious rethinking".

On the question of media having become a trendy affair like showbiz or fashion over the years, about 65 % respondents say the change has been there because the owners have so desired. "A lot of money is involved and a desire to top the TRP ratings is the reason", reasons E4 (Mumbai). "Yes. Total consumerism and big money is all that have led to it", opines R 11(Chandigrah).

An overwhelming majority of respondents preferred a much more diffused pattern of media ownership over a typically concentrated ownership (in the hands of few individuals only). "Diffused ownership would be preferable", writes N4 (Imphal). Similarly C10 (Mumbai) prefers "unity in diversity" to promote and maintain political and cultural pluralism of the country. To the question what they thought of media plurality in a vibrant society, a unanimous "Good" was the response from all respondents.

To the question whether the Government should issue guidelines from time to time to ensure the diversity of media outlets and their content, 90% (108) respondents felt such guidelines should be in place. However, 40% (48) of the respondents opined that Government should not actively meddle into the issue and media should self impose such guidelines. "I would support a regulatory body not supported by the Government", suggests E2 (Mumbai). "Government should have such laws in practice but these should not tamper with the basic freedom of speech and expression", says E5 (New Delhi). All the respondents said "yes" to a related question that when media is concentrated into few hands only, if affects the content and portrayal of events. "Yes, the ideology of those few people who control the media is obvious in anything produced out of their outlets", says C3 (New Delhi).

To the question whether media presently is going through a phase of Murdochisation, 80% (96) respondents said yes, some even gave examples. On another related question about preserving the diversity of media ownership, 65% (78) respondents had a ready answer of following the BBC model. 71.6% (86) respondents, in response to another question, supported the concept of providing a level playing field for small newspapers against big, multi edition groups to maintain parity in competition. "Small newspapers have a big role to play", writes R6 (Mumbai).

All the respondents had a unanimous "yes" to the question that foreign channels have brought with them a new fashion stylebook. A comparison of content and presentation some 20 years ago is a vivid proof of it, they contend. But for many (31%) the change was for better. "It's a matter of demand and supply. So why not!!!" opines R2 (New Delhi). "It is nice to see fresh faces, new trends, new dress code etc.", writes E3 (Bangalore). "Yes, and for the better", writes N6 (Srinagar). "This was well thought out strategy by owners to get noticed by advertisers", comments N8 (Mumbai). "Beauty pageants, fashion shows, lifestyle events etc., are the regular ingredients of news format of present day unlike earlier times", N8 adds.

Generalising the findings, a broad-spectrum of issues concerning the media fraternity came to fore during the survey *(Table 08)*. Firstly, all the respondents were aware of the issues or problems raised in the questionnaire and every respondent, without any exception, had a positive and participatory approach towards the survey.

That 80 per cent of the respondents vouched for a diffused type of media ownership makes a definitive case for ensuring media plurality and checking ownership concentration in the media. The respondents were quick to point out the impact of ownership (of any kind) on the content churned out. They believed that media pluralism is good for a vibrant society.

Table 08
Some Conclusions from the Survey

• Media pluralism good for vibrant society. Ownership is reflected in content.
• Diffused ownership a preferred choice over concentrated one for an overwhelming majority.
• To maintain diversity Government should issue guidelines from time to time, 90% respondents were unanimous. But 45% of respondents say the guidelines should be self-imposing and the Government should not meddle in the issue.
• Foreign channels have brought with them a new fashion stylebook, all agree. But for many (31%) the change was for good.
• Follow the BBC model (65%); allow a level playing field for small newspapers (72%) were some of the suggestions to preserve media diversity as a majority (80%) of respondents agreed that presently media was going through a phase of Murdochisation.

To maintain diversity and diffused character of media ownership all the respondents agreed that the Government from time to time should issue guidelines in this regard. This showed the need for such guidelines at the level of working professionals in the field. But 45% of respondents advising against any Government intervention in this connection also exhibits the need for a self-regulatory mechanism or a regulatory body (Broadcasting Regulatory Authority of India, as proposed in the Broadcast Bill) comprising mostly professionals from the field. Government intervention having proved futile elsewhere, here is not an isolated case.

These findings have revealed the need for diversity and plurality of media ownership in the country. The respondents also highlighted the influence of ownership over the content generated.

That brings us to broad and general observations and conclusions of the study which are listed in the next chapter.

Keys

E1, E2, E3...= Editors/Managing Editors, Executive Editors etc.

N1, N2, N3…= News Producers, Associate Editors and Assistant Editors.

C1, C2, C3…= Chief Copy Desk, Principal Correspondents and Special Correspondents.

R1, R2, R3…= Reporters, Chief Reporters, Sub Editors, Correspondents and Anchors etc.

CHAPTER – EIGHT

Conclusions

The field survey in previous chapter has served to reinforce the earlier theoretical discussions about the consequences of Cross Media Ownership in the country. This has led us to draw some general observations and conclusions about the subject and suggest some possible recommendations to address the same.

These conclusions and recommendations are enumerated in this chapter. Put together, these conclusions range from a worldview scenario on the subject to the prevalent situation in the country in this regard. The conclusions, observations and recommendations are as under:

i) Cross Media restrictions are in place in a number of countries across the globe. This includes some technologically advanced countries like the United States, Japan, England, Italy, etc. Modes of operation, extent and manifestations of these restrictions, however, vary from country to country (Detailed analyses of these restrictions on media ownership in a number of industrialized countries discussed in previous chapters).

ii) In India the study has found two strong but diametrically opposite points of view on the subject. One point of view favours the curbs and the other is against any curbs.

Cross media curbs are unrealistic and against public sentiment. "Disallowing newspapers in television will restrict plurality and diversity of viewers' choice" was the general opinion propounded by the adherents of no-cross-media-curbs school of thought.

Allowing newspapers to diversify into other forms of electronic media would lead to their monopolising the entire market to such an extent that public would be deprived of plurality and diversity of news, views and information, maintained the pro-cross-media-curbs school of thought.

iii) On the legislative front, the Government of India is yet to come up with a law or bill on the subject. In 2007, the federal Congress led Government, however, did prepare a draft Broadcast Bill again, envisaging a middle path on the issue, that of selective regulation. But the bill (Broadcasting Services Regulation Bill-2007) lapsed as it could not be tabled in the Indian parliament. The bill proposed an equity cap of 20% on all cross media holdings. Any media company investing in any other stream of media, other than the one it is already engaged in, should not put in money more than 20% of its total outlay, the bill proposed.

The bill contained almost similar provisions pertaining to Cross Media Ownership as were contained in the previous bill of 1997. But then again it could not be tabled as before that the Government of the day fell.

iv) India's National Media Policy is under change. The First Press Commission (1954) and Second Press Commission (1982) opposed the entry of foreign players into country's media industry. This was also in line with the decision of the Union Cabinet in 1955 disallowing any foreign investment in press in India.

However, with changing times and coming in of economic liberalization, these guidelines also melted away gradually. When almost all sectors of Indian economy were thrown open to foreign investment by the Government, Media industry could not be left behind.

At present there is 100 percent Foreign Direct Investment (FDI) permitted in sectors like Films, advertising, market research, public relations and television through the automatic route. In case of DTH and Cable networks FDI to the extent of 49 percent is allowed while as in case of FM radio it is up to 26%.

In print media, FDI to the tune of 100 percent is allowed in non-news publication categories like scientific, technical journals etc while as 26% FDI is permitted in news and current affairs category.

v) As a result, the I& B Ministry has cleared several titles in news and current affairs category, 115 scientific and technical titles and 180 Indian editions of foreign specialty publications for the FDI. By the same date, 05 titles in news and current affairs category, 09 scientific and technical titles and 18 Indian editions of foreign specialty publications were under the consideration of the Government for the purpose.

This has brought home capital equity to the tune of Rs 19,197.30 crore from April 2000 to February 2015.

vi) Interestingly, ownership concentration in advertising world is strikingly prevalent in the country. The consolidation among the front-runner companies is at its peak. At present there are *Hindustan Thompson Associates* (HTA), *Mudra Communications Ltd., McCann-Erickson India Ltd, Ogilvy & Mather Ltd.* and *Rediffusion –DY&R* working as major players in this Rs. 41, 400 crore industry. The world's largest agglomeration, the US $ 40 billion *Interpublic Group,* plans to consolidate the buying power of all its Indian agencies with an integrated media service unit called Magna Global which will represent the aggregate media negotiating interests of *Interpublic's* Indian entities.

The world's second largest ad agency, WPP formed *Mindshare,* which brings together four of India's top ad agencies. Given such developments, it would seem likely, that not before too long, media buying power in India will be in the hands of two major players, each sharing a substantial transnational base, along with three smaller groups.

It throws up an interesting paradox. The panel of Secretaries, which framed the broad contours of Broadcast Bill in 1997, had recommended lowering of equity of advertising industry in the broadcast medium from the present slab of 20%. But with these corporate mergers making history in the recent past, an altogether different scenario has been thrown up.

vii) A survey conducted on the subject by the author came out with interesting results. 80% of the respondents preferred a diffused ownership over a concentrated one. 90% of the respondents believed Government should issue guidelines from time to time in this regard.

However, 45% respondents felt the guidelines should be self-imposing and the Government should not have a role in thrusting them.

viii) The survey concluded that foreign television channels in the country have brought with them a new culture, a new fashion stylebook. But about 31% of respondents believed the change was for the good.

ix) On the execution front, Cross Media limits can be exercised and enforced on the ground in the following ways:

a) *<u>Percent age wise/Equity:</u>*

This is how the issue has been addressed in the Broadcast Bill of 2007. An overall blanket limit of, say, 15 per cent, 20 per cent or less or more of the equity can be thought over. Here, we look at the overall equity participation of the media concern regardless of its circulation, impact or market share.

b) *<u>Market share (Readership/Viewership/Circulation) in a particular territory/area</u>*

One of the alternatives to equity limits could be market share in a particular territory, area or zone. Here media outlets can be distinguished into three groups depending on the market share in a particular city/town. For newspapers, with less than 33% market share in a particular city/town, wanting to invest in a news channel there should be no equity curbs. Those newspapers whose market share is between 34 and 49 per cent should be allowed to hold up to 49 per cent stake in a news channel in the same city/town.

And those newspapers whose market shares are 50 per cent and above should not be allowed to hold more than 33 per cent stake in a news channel in the same town/city.

It may be better to use the market share concept(either in terms of circulation or readership or both) rather than the equity cap concept.

x) There is a dire need of a national level authority to regulate and oversee a growing cross media interests in the country. There are, though, already bodies like Press Council of India, Telecom Regulatory Authority of India (TRAI) etc. but these bodies either have a limited mandate or are mere recommendatory ones. The regulatory authority, which must be a blend of Press Council and TRAI in terms of reference and scope, is all that is needed to monitor the functioning of cross media units, their circulation and market share, their TRPs, mergers and tie ups, content and other related issues on a full-time basis.

References

A New Future for Communication, Department of Trade and Industry and Department of Culture, Media and Sport, CM 5010, The Stationery Office, London, 2000 (*http://www.statistics.gov.uk/StatBase/Product.asp*, site accessed on May 18, 2004).

Administrative Staff College of India, Report, *Cross Media Ownership in India*, Hyderabad, 2009.

Agashe, J. D. and Mullick, Ashish, 'Are Cross Media Cuts Necessary', The Sunday Times, New Delhi, p-12, November 9, 1997.

Albarran, Alan B., Mierzejewska, Bozena I., *Media Concentration in the U. S. and European Union: A Comparative Analysis*, Journal of Media Economics, Montréal, Canada, May 12-15, 2004.

Amarjit, Mahajan, *Family & Television*, Gyan Publishing House, New Delhi, 1993.

Annual Report, Department of Culture, Media and Sport, CM 5423, The Stationery Office, London, 2000.

Annual Reports, Ministry of Information and Broadcasting, New Delhi, March 31, 2003, 2006, 2011.

Annual Report, Press Council of India, New Delhi, 2007.

Arya, Deepak, '*Branding the print line*', Business Standard, p-8, New Delhi, May 21, 1997.

Arya, Deepak, '*The Imprint of Survival*', Business Standard, p-8, New Delhi, May 20, 1997.

Arya, Deepak, '*The writing on the wall*', Business Standard, p-8, New Delhi, May 22, 1997.

Bagchi, Pradipta and Roy, Rajashi, '*A war in your living room*', The Times of India, p-4, New Delhi, March 19, 2003.

Bagdikian, Ben H., *The Media Monopoly* (4th ed.), Beacon Press, Boston, 1992.

Bahl, Taru, '*Press goes to Town*', The Pioneer, p-12, New Delhi, July 15, 1996.

Basu, D. D., *Constitution of India*, (18th Edition), Prentice Hall of India, New Delhi, 1997.

Bhat, Vignesh N., *Mind Managers & Defiled Doordarshan,* ABS Publishers, Jullundhar, 1987.

Bindu, '*Zero Sum Game*', The Sunday Pioneer, p-12, New Delhi, April 4, 1999.

Bamzai, Kaveree, '*Media tightens its Belt*', The Indian Express, p-3, New Delhi, February 7, 1998,.

Banker, Ashok, '*Star's Final Onslaught*', Outlook, p-21, New Delhi, March 15, 1999.

BECTU, *Review of Cross Media Ownership*, Submission to the Department of Natural History (DNH), London, 1994.

BJP, Party Draft Paper on the media policy, New Delhi, 2007.

BMIG (British Media Industry Group), *A New Approach to Cross Media Ownership,* submission to the DNH, London, 1995.

Bowker, *Broadcasting and Cable Yearbook*, New Jersey, 2003.

Broadcasting Services Regulation Bill-2007 (Draft), Ministry of Information & Broadcasting, New Delhi, 2007.

Browne, Christopher, *The Prying Game: The Sex, Sleaze and Scandals of Fleet Street and the Media Mafia,* Robson Books Ltd., London, 1996.

Butcher, Melissa, *Transnational Television, Cultural Identity & Change—When STAR came to India*, Sage, New Delhi, 2003.

Burman, Rachna, '*Surviving the Odds*', The Pioneer, p-12, New Delhi, January 6, 1998.

Business Standard, '*Media to see increase in FDI*', New Delhi, p-3, June 22, 2006.

Chakravarti, Avijit, '*Bodies of Evidence*', The Pioneer, p-12, New Delhi, April 4, 1999.

Chakarvarty, Jaya, *Women in Media*, Vol-I & II, Swarup and Sons, New Delhi, 2002.

Chakravarty, Suhas, *Press & Media-The Global Dimension*, Kanishka Publishers, New Delhi, 1997.

Chatterji, P. C., *Broadcasting in India*, Sage, New Delhi, 1987.

Chaturvedi, Swati, SAB TV, interview with, New Delhi, September 30, 2004.

Chintala, Medha, *'Cross-Media Companies are on the Rise'* on *www.indianmba. com/Faculty_Column*, Hyderabad, 2008(Site accessed on May 16, 2008).

Citation, *Rights and Duties of the Editor*, Association of Norwegian Editors, Oslo, October 22, 1953(Revised 1973).

Coleridge, N., *Paper Tigers*, Mandarin, London, 1993.

Collins, R. and Murroni, C., *New Media, New Policies: Media and Communication Strategies for the Future*, Polity Press, Cambridge, 1996.

Committee of Experts on Media Concentrations and Pluralism (MM-CM), report on Media Concentrations and Pluralism in Europe, Strasbourg, 1997.

Consolidated FDI Policy, Department of Industrial Policy and Promotion, Ministry of Commerce and Industry, Government of India, New Delhi, 2015.

Corporate Bureau, *'Broadcast law Okayed'*, Business Standard, p-2, New Delhi, April 30, 1997.

Country Report, *Mapping Digital Media: India*, Open Society Foundations, New Delhi, 2013.

Dalal, Sucheta, *'Media Houses tapping issue Market,'* The Times of India, p-14, Bombay, August 20, 1995.

Das, Kankana, *'New age space selling'*, The Pioneer, p-5, New Delhi, July 10, 1997.

Dasgupta, Abhijit, *'Titans clash over price slash'*, The Pioneer, p-4, Calcutta, July 24, 1997.

Dinan, W., *The Republic of Ireland's Media Space: Ownership, Regulation and Policy*, Stirling Media Research Institute Report, Stirling, 2001.

DNH, *Media Ownership: The Government's Proposals*, CM 2872, HMSO, London, May 1995.

Doyle, Gillian, *'From Pluralism to Media Ownership: Europe's emergent policy on media concentrations,'* Journal of Information Law and Technology, London, 1997.

Doyle, Gillian, *Media Ownership - The Economic and Policy Convergence*, Sage, London, 2002.

Doyle, Gillian, '*Regulation of Media Ownership and Pluralism in Europe: Can the European Union take us Forward?*', Cardozo Arts & Entertainment Law Journal, 16(2-3): 451-473, London, 1998.

Doyle, Gillian, '*Towards a pan-European directive? From concentration and pluralism to media ownership*', Journal of Communication Law, 3(1): London, November 15, 1998.

Dutta, R. S., '*Newspapers, then and now*', The Tribune, p-12, New Delhi, September 19, 1996.

First Press Commission, report, pp. 272, New Delhi, 1954.

FICCI – PricewaterhouseCoopers, Report, *Indian Entertainment and Media Industry – A Growth Story Unfolds*, New Delhi, 2006.

FICCI-KPMG, Reports, *Indian Media & Entertainment Industry*, New Delhi, 2014, 2015, 2016.

Foreign Investment Policy, Circular, Ministry of Information and Broadcasting, Government of India, New Delhi, 2003.

French, David and Richards, Michael (Eds.): *Contemporary Television, Contemporary Perspective*, Sage, New Delhi, 1997.

French, David and Richards, Michael (Eds.): *Television in Contemporary Asia*, Sage, New Delhi, 2000.

Garnham, Nicholas, *Capitalism & Communication-Global Culture and Economics of Information*, London, Sage, 1990.

Gatzen, Barbara, '*Public broadcasting, media ownership and democratic debate in Japan*' on *http://www.opendemocracy.net/media-globalmediaownership*, 2002(Site accessed on September 12, 2007).

Ghosh, Pothick, *The colour of money*, The Pioneer, p-11, New Delhi, September 26, 1996.

Golding, Peter, *Communicating Politics-Mass Communication & Political Process*, Leicester University Press, London, 1998.

Goldsmith, Jill and Dawatrey, Adam, '*Murdoch: Sky's the limit*', Variety, pp. 1, 130, London, 28 August-03 September 2000.

Goyal, S. K., and Rao, Challaphathi, *Ownership and Control Structure of the Indian Press*, Public Printing and Planning Division, Indian Institute of Public Administration, New Delhi, February 1981.

Guidelines for up linking of News Channels, Circular Ministry of Information & Broadcasting, Government of India, New Delhi, March 26, 2003.

Guidelines for foreign investment, Circular Ministry of Information & Broadcasting, Government of India, New Delhi, March 31, 2006.

Gunaratne, Shelton A., *Handbook of the Media in Asia,* Sage, New Delhi, 2000.

Gupta, V. S. and Dayal, Rajeshwar, *National Media Policy,* Concept, New Delhi, 1996.

Guth, Dorothy Lobrano, *Letters of E. B. White,* Harper & Row, New York, 1976.

Harding, J., *'Pearson and Li group to announce alliance in Asia',* Financial Times, London, July 3, 2000.

Hargreaves, D., *'New media, new rules',* Financial Times, p-14, London, July 7, 2000.

Hirsch, M. and Petersen, V., *'European Policy Initiatives'* in Mc. Quail, Denis and Suine, Karen (ed.), *Media Policy—Convergence, Concentration and Commerce,* Euromedia Research Group, Sage, London, 1998.

Hukill, Mark and Vallath, Chandarshekar, *Electronic Communication Convergence - Policy Challenges in Asia,* Sage, New Delhi, 2002.

Humphreys, Peter J., *Mass Media and Media Policy in Western Europe,* Manchester University Press, Manchester, 1996.

India-2003, Publications Division, Ministry of Information and Broadcasting, Government of India, New Delhi, 2004.

Indian Federation of Working Journalists, *India's Monopoly Press- a Mirror of Distortion-1973,* New Delhi, 1974.

International Journal of Communication, Bahri Publications, Vol. 13, No. 1, p.45-54, New Delhi, Dec 2002-Jan 2003.

Jacob, Rahul, *'Star is shooting towards interactive TV',* Financial Times, p.11, London, June 10-11, 2000.

Jeffrey, Robin, *India's Newspaper Revolution –Capitalism, Politics and the Indian language Press-1977-99,* Oxford University Press, New Delhi/Melbourne, 2001.

Jindal, Vijay, *'Weigh Profit Against Pride',* India Today, p- 27, New Delhi, June 30, 1997.

Journal of Communication, Vol. 52, No. 2, p.34, Oxford University Press, London, June 2002.

Kang, Bhavdeep, *'Read the Fine Print'*, Outlook, p-37, New Delhi, July 8, 2002.

Karkaria, Bachi, Editor, *The Times of India*, interview with, New Delhi, April 5, 2004.

Karkaria, Bachi, *'Politics, business rule media bash'*, The Times of India, 14, New Delhi, June, 11, 2003.

Khan, Moinuddin, *'Foreign Investment in Print Media'*, Urdu Duniya, p-12, New Delhi, September 2002.

Kleinwachter, *'W. Germany'* in D. Goldberg, T. Prosser and S. Verhulst(Eds.), *Regulating the Changing Media*, Oxford University Press, London, 1998.

Kohli, Payal, Editor, *Cosmopolitan*, interview with, New Delhi, April 5, 2006.

Kohli, Vanita, *The Indian Media Business*, Sage, New Delhi, 2005, 2010.

Kohli, Vanita, *'The Making of India's Biggest Media House'*, Businessworld, p-7, June 2, 2003, New Delhi.

Kumar, Anand, Department of Global Studies, JNU, interview with, New Delhi, March 24, 2006.

Kumar, Dinesh, *'Gimmicks to sell magazines'*, The Pioneer, p-11, New Delhi, February 26, 1996.

Kumar, Keval J., *Mass Communication in India*, Jaico, Pune, 2008.

Kumari, Abhilasha, *Media the key driver of consumerism*, Institute of Studies in Industrial Development, New Delhi, 2008.

MacLeod, V (Ed.)., *Media Ownership and Control in the Age of Convergence*, International Institute of Communications, London, 1996.

Madhav, Tushar, *Media: Whose piper, whose tune* on *http://www.merinews.com*, New Delhi, 2008(Site accessed on April 16, 2008).

Mass Media in India, Publications Division, Ministry of Information & Broadcasting, New Delhi, 2003.

Mathur, W.D., *Community Radio Broadcasting*, Ministry of Information & Broadcasting, New Delhi, July 10, 2003.

Mc. Quail, Denis and Suine, Karen (ed.), *Media Policy—Convergence, Concentration and Commerce,* Euromedia Research Group, Sage, London, 1998.

McChesney, Robert W., *Rich Media, Poor Democracy: Communication Politics in Dubious Times*, The New Press, New York, 2000.

Mehta, Nalin, *Behind A Billion Screens: What Television Tells Us About Modern India,* Harper Collins, New Delhi, 2015.

Meier, W. A., and Trappel, J., *Media Concentration and the public interest*, Euromedia Research Group, Sage, London, 1998.

Melkote, Srinivas, Shields, Phillip and Agarwal, Binod S(Eds.), *International Satellite Television in South Asia*, University Press of America, New York, 1998.

Mitra, Anjan, '*The Weekly War*', Business Standard, p-3, New Delhi, June 12, 1997.

Moily, Veerapa, Chairperson, AICC Media Cell, interview with, New Delhi, August 25, 2007.

Mukul, Akshay, '*Moving on to a new track*', The Pioneer, p-7, New Delhi, August 28, 1995.

Mullick, Ashish, '*Cross Media curbs unrealistic...*', The Times of India, p-9, New Delhi, Nov 8, 1997.

Mullick, Ashok, *We expect Indian media market...(*interview with Grindon, Michael), The Times of India, New Delhi, April 14, 2003.

Murdock, G. and Golding, P., '*Capitalism, communication and class relations*', in J. Curran, M. Gurevitch and J. Woollacott(eds), *Mass Communication and Society*, Edward Arnold, London, 1977.

Muthiah, Hepzi, '*The new media mantra*', The Asian Age, p-11, New Delhi, June 23, 1997.

Muthiah, Hepzi, '*Subhash Chandra-Catches a flying star*', The Asian Age, p-19, New Delhi, October 10, 1999.

Nathan, Joseph, Editorial Advisor, Asia Pacific Communication Associates (APCA), interview with, New Delhi, September 27, 2006.

Newspaper Society, *Submission to the Culture, Media and Sport Select Committee and to the DTI and DCMS*, London, 2004.

NI, *Response to the White Paper, A New Future for Communications*, London, 2004.

Nicholas, John and McChesney, Robert W., *It's the Media, Stupid*, Seven Stories Press, New York, 2000.

Ninan, Sevanti, *Headlines from the Heartland*, Sage, New Delhi, 2007.

Noorani, A.G., '*Foreign and Indian Media*', The Kashmir Times, p-7, Jammu, March 17, 2008.

NUJ, *Cross Media Ownership: A Submission to the National Heritage Ministry by the National Union of Journalists*, NUJ, London, 1994.

Padgaonkar, Dileep, Chairman, Asia Pacific Communication Associates (APCA), interview with, New Delhi, April 12, 2007.

Page, David and Crawlley, William, *Satellite over South Asia*, Sage, New Delhi, 2001.

Pande, Bhanu and Shukla, Seema, *'Big Brother is Watching'*, The Economic Times-Brand Equity, p-1, New Delhi, April 9, 2003.

Pandey, Rama, Freelance Television producer, interview with, Jammu, April 24, 2006.

Pearson, plc, *Submission to the DNH on Cross Media Ownership Rules*, Pearson, London, 1994.

Pogrebin, Robin, *'The New Yorker Rolls, but ads lag'*, The Times of India, p-3, New Delhi, October 20, 1996.

'Power of the Foreign Press', Combat Law, Vol. 2, No. 1, p-39, Mumbai, April-May, 2003.

Prabhaker, Nawal, *Media & Communication, Vol-I, Commonwealth Publishers*, New Delhi, 1998.

Prabhaker, Nawal, *Media & Communication, Vol-II, Commonwealth Publishers*, New Delhi, 1998.

Prasad, H. Y. Sharda, *'A licence to print one's own money'*, The Asian Age, p-11, New Delhi, October 14, 1997.

Prasad, Nandini, *A Vision Unveiled*, Har-Anand Publishers, New Delhi, 1994.

Press Council of India, *Future of Print Media-A Report*, New Delhi, 2001.

Price, Monroe, Rozumilowicz, Beata and Verhulst, Stefaan G., *Media Reform: Democratizing the Media, Democratizing the State*, Routledge, New York, 2002.

Prosser, T., Goldberg, D. and Verhulst, S., (Eds.), *The Impact of New Communication Technologies on Media Concentrations and Pluralism*, University of Glasgow, London, 1996.

Prothi, Rajesh, India Editor, *Telecom Asia*, interview with, New Delhi, September 29, 2005.

Punnen, P. C., *'A question of credibility'*, The Pioneer, p-11, New Delhi, August 7, 1995.

Raman, Anuradha, *'Down with the count'*, Outlook, p- 6, New Delhi, May 6-12, 2008.

Rao, Bhaskara, *'A few reasonable restrictions only'*, The Pioneer, p-11, New Delhi, September 9, 1997.

Rao, Bhaskara and Vasanti, P.N., *Media Scene as India Globalises*, Centre for Media Studies, New Delhi, 2006.

Rao, Sandhya and Melkote, Srinivas R., *Critical Issues in Communication-Looking Inward for Answers,* Sage, New Delhi, 2001.

RNI, *Press in India* (44[th,] 49th, 50th, 51st, 58th and 59th) Annual Reports for 1999-2000, 2004-05, 2005-06, 2006-07, 2013-14, 2014-15, New Delhi, 2015.

Rhaguvanshi, Manoj, *'Khula Manch'*, SAB TV, New Delhi, July 13, 2003.

Sarkar, Bidyut, *'A case for Cross Media Ownership'*, The Times of India, p-7, New Delhi, July 31, 1997.

Sarkar, Chanchal, *'Has Media Liberalisation a Price'*, Mainstream, p-7, New Delhi, March 29, 1997.

Sarma, Ratna, *'Newspapers need a strategy for survival'*, The Times of India, p-3, New Delhi, June 26, 1997.

'Satellite TV poses no threat', The Hindu, p-2, Bombay, October 18, 1995.

Saxena, Jagdeep, *'Direct to Home'*, Rashtriya Sahara, p- 11, Lucknow, November 19, 2000.

Saxena, Poonam, *'I believe in long term investment'*, The Pioneer, p-11, New Delhi, May 13, 1997.

Second Press Commission, report, New Delhi, 1982.

Sengupta, Nitish, interview of, *'Check on Cross Media holdings'*, Observer of Business and Politics, p-3, New Delhi, March 14, 1997.

Sharma, P. V., *Radio-Television & Elections*, Concept, New Delhi, 1998.

SIMCON-XXVI (26th State Information Ministers' Conference), deliberations of, on Broadcast Bill, New Delhi, September 19-20, 2007.

Singh, Tavleen, *'Fourth Estate Bandaging'*, The Indian Express, p-3, New Delhi, July 31, 1995.

Singh, Vikas, *'Clear Signals'* (Interview with I&B Minister Ravi Shanker Prasad), The Times of India, p-12, New Delhi, June 11, 2003.

Singhal, Arvind and Rogers, Everelte, *Indian Communication Revolution: From Bullock Carts to Cyber Marts,* Sage, New Delhi, 2001.

Sinha, Bharti, *'Secretaries Panel in favour of media cross holdings'*, Business Standard, p-2, New Delhi, February 22, 1997.

Soni, Ambika, Minister for I&B, speech at 3rd All India Editors Conference, Srinagar, October 13, 2009.

Special Correspondent, *'Plea to end Cross-media ownership'*, The Pioneer, p-4, New Delhi, March 30, 1996.

Sridhar, V., *'Broadcasters at war'*, Frontline, p-69, Chennai, August 15, 2003.

Srivastava, K.M., *Media in 21ˢᵗ Century*, Stirling Publishers, New Delhi, 1998.

Swarup, Asha, Secretary, I&B Ministry, interview with, New Delhi, September 18, 2007.

Telecom Regulatory Authority of India (TRAI), Consultation Paper No. 13/2008 on Media Ownership, New Delhi, September 23, 2008.

Telecom Regulatory Authority of India (TRAI), Consultation Paper No. 01/2013 on Issues relating to Media Ownership, New Delhi, February 15, 2013.

Thakurta, Paranjoy Guha, *Media ownership trends in India* on *http://thehoot.org/web/MediaownershiptrendsinIndia/6053-1-1-16-true.html*, July 03, 2012, New Delhi.

The Economic Times, *'Murdock to call all shots'*, p-3, New Delhi, July 31, 2003.

The Economist, *'Star turn'*, pp. 67-68, New York, March 11, 2000.

The Hindu, *'No more FDI in media: CPI'*, p-6, New Delhi, January 24, 2006.

The Times of India, *'I haven't done anything to invite hatred: Big B'*, New Delhi, p-7, June 08, 2008.

The Times of India News Service, *'Strategic Alliance and Necessity for Media'*, The Times of India, p-7, Chennai, September 4, 1997.

Thomas, Sunil K., *'India's Air War'*, The Week, p-22, New Delhi, April 13, 2003.

Thomas, Pradip, *Media Ownership & Communication Rights in India*, Zed Publishers, London, 2004.

Thomas, Pradip and Zoharam, Nain(Eds.), *Who owns the Media—Global Trends and the Local Resistances*, WACC and Zed Publishers, London, 2004.

Thomas, Pradip, N., *Political Economy of Communications in India: The Good, the Bad and the Ugly*, Sage, New Delhi, 2010.

Times News Network, *'Star gets breather'*, The Times of India, p-5, New Delhi, March 27, 2003.

Tiwari, Maneesh, Spokesperson, All India Congress Committee, interview with, New Delhi, June 05, 2007.

Tribune News Service, *'Newspapers must check invasion from skies'*, The Tribune, p-3, Shimla, September 16, 1996.

UK- 2003, the official Yearbook of United Kingdom, Government of UK, London, 2004.

Uniyal, Shardah, *'Managing the media'*, Observer of Business and Politics, p-5, New Delhi, March 14, 1998.

Vakil, Dina, *'TV poses no threat'*, The Times of India, p-12, Amsterdam, July 29, 1995.

White, Aiden, *Journalism and the War on Terrorism*, International Federation of Journalists, Paris, 2002.

Williams, G., *Evidence to Cross Media Ownership-Review Submitted by the Campaign for Press and Broadcasting Freedom*, CPBF, London, 1994.

Yadav, J. S. and Mathur, Pradeep, *Issues in Mass Communication,* Vol-I & II, Kanishka Publishers, New Delhi, 1998.

Websites	Accessed on
http://www.bjp.org	Aug 28, 2007
http://www.bestmediainfo.com/2014/03/ficci-kpmg-prjcts	May 22, 2014
http://www.cmsindia.org/roundtable	Feb 05, 2008
http://www.opsi.gov.uk/acts/acts2003/ukpga_20030021_en_1	April 02, May 23, 2004
http://conclave.digitaltoday.in/conclave2008	April 27, 2008
http://cpim.org/search/node/Media%20Policies?page=1	August 19, 2007
http://dipp.nic.in/English/policies/FDI_Circular_2015.pdf	June 02, 2015
http://dipp.nic.in/English/Publications/FDI_Statistics/2015/india_FDI_February2015.pdf	July 15, 2015
http://www.democraticmedia.org/resources/reading_list/media_ownership	April 22, 2006; June 09, 2005
http://economictimes.indiatimes.com/articleshow/46269343.cms?utm_source=contentofinterest&utm_medium=text&utm_campaign=cppst	Feb 18, 2015
http://www.ficci.com/media-room.asp	Jan 12, 2008; June 14, 2007
http://www.guardian.co.uk/media	Jan 27, 2008
http://indiatoday.digitaltoday.in	Feb21, 2008
http://www.indiatimes.com/aboutus.cms	April 17, Aug 18, 2006; July 24, 2005
http://www.indiatogether.org	Nov 05, 2010; Sept 11, 2007
http://www.livemint.com/Companies/hzwX3zKAVEL1g8SQgxFCWM/html	August 18, 2012
http://www.mib.nic.in/bills	Aug 25, 2008; July 27, Aug 11, 2006
http://delhi.meowfm.com/index.php?option=com_content&task=view&id=12&Itemid=27	Sept 08, 2008
http://www.forbes.com/sites/meghabahree/2014/05/30/reliance-takes-over-network18-is-this-the-death-of-media-independence/	July 27, 2015; Dec 22, 2014
http://www.ndtv.com/convergence/ndtv/corporatepage/index.aspx	Jun 07, 2015; Sept. 17, 2014; Oct 09, 2008; June 05, 2006

http/www.opsi.gov.uk/acts/acts2003/ukpga_20030021_en_1	May 25, 2005
http://www.outlookindia.com/article/ the-new-media-moguls/294353	July 13, 2015; Nov 23, 2014
http://www.pib.nic.in/pressreleases	June 24, Oct 07, 2009; Jan 27, 2007
http://www.robertmcchesney.com	Jan 28, 2006; Oct 21, 2005
http://www.scatmag.com/govt.htm	July 27, 2007
http://en.wikipedia.org/wiki/Cross_ownership	Oct 16, 2006

Appendix I

Key transactions in 2014-15

Mergers & Acquisitions

Date	Target name	Target sector	Acquirer name
January 14	Greedy Game Media Pvt. Ltd	Digital	TLabs
February 14	Odigma Consultancy Pvt. Ltd.	Digital	Infibeam Inc.
May 14	Network 18 Media & Investments Ltd.	TV broadcast	Independent Media Trust
May 14	TV 18 Broadcast Limited	TV broadcast	Independent Media Trust
June 14	Temple Advertising Pvt. Ltd	Advertising	Bates CHI &Partners
July 14	Reliance Media Works Ltd.	Post production/ VFX/Graphic design	Prime Focus Ltd.
July 14	HDL Entertainment Pvt. Ltd.	Cinema exhibition	Carnival Films Pvt. Ltd.
July 14	WhatsOn India Media Ltd.	Film/TV production	Tribune Digital Ventures Singapore Pte Ltd.

July 14	Superior Films Pvt. Ltd.	Cinema exhibition	Inax Leisure Ltd.
August 14	Purple Entertainment Ltd., Content Assets	Digital	Global Eagle Entertainment Inc
October 14	Sambhaav Media Ltd	Print	Infotel Televentures Pvt. Ltd.
December 14	NetworkPlay Media Pvt. Ltd.	Advertising	Smile Vun Group Pvt. Ltd.
December 14	BIG Cinemas	Cinema exhibition	Carnival Films Pvt. Ltd.
December 14	Four Lions Films Pvt. Ltd.	Film/TV production	52 Weeks Entertainment Ltd.
December 14	Radio City	Radio and OOH	Dainik Jagran group

PE

January 14	SureWaves MediaTechnologies Pvt. Ltd.	Advertising	Canaan Partners
March 14	Technology Frontiers India Pvt. Ltd.	Advertising	Fidel's World Asset Management
June 14	Bigtree Entertainment Pvt. Ltd.	Digital	Accel Partners, SAIF Partners, Network 18 Media & Investments Ltd.
July 14	Hungama Digital Media Entertainment Pvt. Ltd.	Digital	Bessema Venture Partners; Intel Capital
August 14	Hathway Cable & Datacom Ltd.	TV distribution	Capital Research and Management Company, American Funds Insurance Series-Global Small Capitalisation Fund
August 14	InMobi Technologies Pvt. Ltd.	Advertising	SoftBank Capital
October 14	PVR Ltd.	Cinema exhibition	
December 14	Newgen Imaging Systems Pvt. Ltd.	Digital	The Carlyle Group

January 14	SureWaves MediaTechnologies Pvt. Ltd.	Advertising	Canaan Partners
March 14	Technology Frontiers India Pvt. Ltd.	Advertising	Fidel's World Asset Management
January 15	Videocon D2H	TV broadcast	Silver Eagle Acquisition

Appendix II

List of cases cleared and under consideration for FDI in Media by the Government of India.

LIST OF CASES APPROVED BY I&B MINISTRY

A. Indian edition of foreign scientific/technical/specialty magazines/ journals/periodicals

S.No.	NAME OF THE APPLICANT COMPANY	NAME OF MAGAZINE	DATE OF APPROVAL LETTER
01.	M/s. Living Media India Ltd.	Golf Digest	22nd January 2003
02.	M/s. Living Media India Ltd.	Scientific American (Name changed to Scientific American India)	3rd February 2003 and 25th April 2005
03.	M/s. Living Media India Ltd.	Cosmopolitan	4th July 2003

04.	M/s. Living Media India Ltd.	Reader's Digest	15th September 2003
05.	M/s. Exposure Media Marketing Private Ltd.	Par Golf	15th October 2003
06.	M/s. Prism Books Pvt. Ltd.	The Journal of Antimicrobial Chemotherapy	19th February 2004
07.	M/s. Prism Books Pvt. Ltd.	Human Reproduction	19th February 2004
08.	M/s. Prism Books Pvt. Ltd.	Journal of Dermatological Treatment	19th February 2004
09.	M/s. Exposure Media Marketing Private Ltd.	ASIASPA	19th February 2004
10.	M/s. Living Media India Ltd.	Good Housekeeping	16th April 2004
11.	M/s. Prism Books Pvt. Ltd.	Blood Pressure	16th July 2004
12.	M/s. Prism Books Pvt. Ltd.	Journal of Obstetrics and Gynecology	20th July 2004
13.	M/s. Prism Books Pvt. Ltd.	Hematology	20th July 2004
14.	M/s. Prism Books Pvt. Ltd.	International Journal of Psychiatry in Clinical Practice	20th July 2004
15.	M/s. Prism Books Pvt. Ltd.	UroOncology	29th July 2004
16.	M/s. Prism Books Pvt. Ltd.	Aids Abstracts	17th August 2004
17.	M/s. Quintessence Science Communications Pvt. Ltd.	Quintessence International	17th August 2004
18.	M/s. IBS Publishing Pvt. Ltd.	International Banking System	14th February 2005

19.	M/s. Himalayan International Institute of Yoga Science and Philosophy	Yoga International	21st February 2005
20.	M/s. Fachpresse Publishers Pvt. Ltd.	Printcom India	16th March 2005
21.	M/s. Prism Books Pvt. Ltd.	Clinical Intensive Care	27th April 2005
22.	M/s. Prism Books Pvt. Ltd.	Journal of Cosmetic and laser Therapy	27th April 2005
23.	M/s. Prism Books Pvt. Ltd.	Human Fertility	27th April 2005
24.	M/s. Worldwide Media Ltd.	Top Gear	27th April 2005
25.	M/s. Paprika Media Pvt. Ltd.	Time Out Mumbai	25th May 2005
26.	M/s. Prism Books Pvt. Ltd	Advances in Psychiatric Treatment	1st June 2005
27.	Wholly owned subsidiary of M/s. International Data Group Inc., (IDG), USA	Indian editions of IDG and publication of scientific/technical magazines	16th June 2005
28.	M/s. Prism Books Pvt. Ltd.	Leukemia & Lymphoma	12th July 2005
29.	M/s. Homoeopathic Research & Charities	Homoeopathic Links	12th July 2005
30.	M/s. IDG Media Pvt. Ltd.	CIO	24th August 2005
31.	M/s. Living Media India Ltd.	Men's Health	27th September 2005
32.	M/s. Media Transasia India Ltd.	Maxim	21st October 2005
33.	M/s. Springer India Pvt. Ltd.	World Journal of Urology	18th November 2005

34.	M/s. Next Gen Publishing Ltd.	Car India	28th December 2005
35.	M/s. Media Transasia India Ltd.	Travel & Leisure	9th March 2006
36.	M/s Living Media India Ltd.	Prevention	21st April 2006
37.	M/s Outlook Publishing (India) Pvt. Ltd.	Marie Claire	25th April 2006
38.	M/s. Prism Books Pvt. Ltd.	Journal of Asthma	25th April 2006
39.	M/s. Prism Books Pvt. Ltd.	Annals of Oncology	25th April 2006
40.	M/s. Prism Books Pvt. Ltd.	Brain	27th April 2006
41.	M/s. Conde Nest Asia/ Pacific Inc., USA (M/s. BVA Publisher Pvt. Ltd.)	Vogue	5th June 2006
42.	M/s. Next Gen Publishing Ltd.	Computer Active	8th June 2006
43.	M/s. BVA Publisher Pvt. Ltd.	Glamour India	8th June 2006
44.	M/s. IDG Media Pvt. Ltd.	PC World	23rd June 2006
45.	M/s. GPE Expo Pvt. Ltd.	Pharmaceutical Technology	6th July 2006
46.	M/s VJM Media Pvt. Ltd	OK! INDIA	6th July 2006
47.	M/s. Springer India Pvt. Ltd.	HeRNIa	2nd August 2006
48.	M/s. Springer India Pvt. Ltd.	European Journal of Nutrition	2nd August 2006
49.	M/s. Media Transasia India Ltd.	Better Homes & Garden	14th August 2006
50.	M/s. Springer India Pvt. Ltd.	European Journal of Orthopedic Surgery & Traumatology	18th August 2006

51.	M/s. Springer India Pvt. Ltd.	Intensive Care Medicine	18th August 2006
52.	M/s. Springer India Pvt. Ltd.	International Orthopaedics	18th August 2006
53.	M/s. Springer India Pvt. Ltd.	Lung	18th August 2006
54.	M/s. Springer India Pvt. Ltd.	Infection	18th August 2006
55.	M/s. Springer India Pvt. Ltd.	Journal of Neurology	18th August 2006
56.	M/s. Springer India Pvt. Ltd.	World Journal of Surgery	18th August 2006
57.	M/s. Springer India Pvt. Ltd.	Supportive Care in Cancer	18th August 2006
58.	M/s. Springer India Pvt. Ltd.	European Archives of Oto Rhino Laryngology	18th August 2006
59.	M/s. Springer India Pvt. Ltd.	Archives of Dermatological Research	18th August 2006
60.	M/s Ezyhealth Asia Pacific Ltd	Medical Grapevine	18th August 2006
61.	M/s Prism Books Pvt. Ltd	Annals of Clinical Psychiatry	18th August 2006
62.	M/s Prism Books Pvt. Ltd	British Journal of Neurosurgery	18th August 2006
63.	M/s. Springer India Pvt. Ltd.	Osteoporosis International	18th August 2006
64.	M/s. Springer India Pvt. Ltd.	Diabetologia	18th August 2006
65.	M/s. Springer India Pvt. Ltd.	Basic Research in Cardiology	18th August 2006
66.	M/s. Springer India Pvt. Ltd.	Archives of Orthopaedic and Trauma Surgery	18th August 2006

67.	M/s. Springer India Pvt. Ltd.	Kidney	18th August 2006
68.	M/s. Springer India Pvt. Ltd.	Heart and Vessels	18th August 2006
69.	M/s. Springer India Pvt. Ltd.	Archives of Gynecology and Obstetrics	18th August 2006
70.	M/s. Springer India Pvt. Ltd.	Clinical Rheumatology	18th August 2006
71.	M/s. Springer India Pvt. Ltd.	The Mathematical Intelligencer	18th August 2006
72.	M/s. Springer India Pvt. Ltd.	European Journal of Pediatrics	18th August 2006
73.	M/s. Springer India Pvt. Ltd.	European Spine Journal	18th August 2006
74.	M/s. Springer India Pvt. Ltd.	Disease of Colon & Rectum	18th August 2006
75.	M/s. Springer India Pvt. Ltd.	Pediatric Surgery International	18th August 2006
76.	M/s. Springer India Pvt. Ltd.	Journal of Orthopaedics and Traumatology	18th August 2006
77.	M/s. Springer India Pvt. Ltd.	The Journal of Headache and Pain	18th August 2006
78.	M/s. Springer India Pvt. Ltd.	Graefe's Archive for Clinical and Experimental ophthalmology	18th August 2006
79.	M/s. Living Media India Ltd.	Harvard Business Review South Asia	11th September 2006
80.	M/s. Prism Books Pvt. Ltd.	COPD – Journal of Chronicle Obstructive Pulmonary Disease	19th September 2006
81.	M/s. Wolters Kluwer Health (India) Pvt. Ltd.	Current Opinion in Neurology	22nd September 2006

82.	M/s. Wolters Kluwer Health (India) Pvt. Ltd.	Anesthesia & Analgesia	22nd September 2006
83.	M/s. Wolters Kluwer Health (India) Pvt. Ltd.	Laryngoscope	22nd September 2006
84.	M/s. Wolters Kluwer Health (India) Pvt. Ltd.	Current Opinion Pulmonary Medicine	22nd September 2006
85.	M/s. Wolters Kluwer Health (India) Pvt. Ltd.	Current Opinion in Nephrology & Hypertension	22nd September 2006
86.	M/s. Wolters Kluwer Health (India) Pvt. Ltd.	Current Opinion in Obstetrics & Gynecology	22nd September 2006
87.	M/s. Wolters Kluwer Health (India) Pvt. Ltd.	Neurology	22nd September 2006
88.	M/s. Wolters Kluwer Health (India) Pvt. Ltd.	Anesthesiology	22nd September 2006
89.	M/s. Wolters Kluwer Health (India) Pvt. Ltd.	Neurologist	22nd September 2006
90.	M/s. Wolters Kluwer Health (India) Pvt. Ltd.	Current Opinion in Urology	22nd September 2006
91.	M/s. Reed Infomedia India Pvt. Ltd	"Control Engineering"	22nd September 2006
92.	M/s. Reed Infomedia India Pvt. Ltd	"Flight International"	22nd September 2006
93.	M/s. Reed Infomedia India Pvt. Ltd	"Logistics Management"	22nd September 2006
94.	M/s. Reed Infomedia India Pvt. Ltd	"JCK"	22nd September 2006
95.	M/s Worldwide Media Pvt. Ltd.	Hello	14th November 2006
96.	M/s. Indian Dental Association	The Journal of the American Dental Association	24th November 2006
97.	M/s. Worldwide Media Pvt. Ltd.	Grazia	24th November 2006

98.	M/s. Springer (India) Pvt. Ltd.	Clinical and Experimental Medicine	6th December 2006
99.	M/s. Springer (India) Pvt. Ltd.	Surgical Endoscopy	6th December 2006
100.	M/s. Springer (India) Pvt. Ltd.	Digestive Diseases and Sciences	6th December 2006
101.	M/s. Springer (India) Pvt. Ltd.	Heart Failure Reviews	6th December 2006
102.	M/s. Springer (India) Pvt. Ltd.	European Clinics Obstetrics and Gynecology	6th December 2006
103.	M/s. Springer (India) Pvt. Ltd.	European Journal of Plastic Surgery	6th December 2006
104.	M/s. Springer (India) Pvt. Ltd.	Langenbeck's Archives of Surgery	6th December 2006
105.	M/s. Springer (India) Pvt. Ltd.	Pain Digest	6th December 2006
106.	M/s. Springer (India) Pvt. Ltd.	International Journal of Colorectal Disease	6th December 2006
107.	M/s. Springer (India) Pvt. Ltd.	Psychiatric Quarterly	6th December 2006
108.	M/s. Springer (India) Pvt. Ltd.	Esophagus	6th December 2006
109.	M/s Next Gen Publishing Limited	FHM	5th February 2007
110.	M/s Planman Media Pvt. Ltd.	The Indian PC Magazine	23rd March 2007
111.	M/ Exposure Media Marketing Pvt. Ltd.	Millionaire Asia	2nd April 2007
112.	M/s Wolters Kluwer Health (India) Pvt. Ltd.	The Clinical Journal of Pain	3rd April 2007
113.	M/s Wolters Kluwer Health (India) Pvt. Ltd.	Current Opinion in Internal Medicine	3rd April 2007

114.	M/s Wolters Kluwer Health (India) Pvt. Ltd.	Current Opinion in Rheumatology	3rd April 2007
115.	M/s Wolters Kluwer Health (India) Pvt. Ltd.	Annals of Surgery	3rd April 2007
116.	M/s Wolters Kluwer Health (India) Pvt. Ltd.	Current Opinion in Lipidology	3rd April 2007
117.	M/s Wolters Kluwer Health (India) Pvt. Ltd.	AIDS	3rd April 2007
118.	M/s Wolters Kluwer Health (India) Pvt. Ltd.	European Journal of Gastroenterology & Hepatology	3rd April 2007
119.	M/s Wolters Kluwer Health (India) Pvt. Ltd.	Journal of Clinical Gastroenterology	3rd April 2007
120.	M/s Reed Infomedia India Pvt. Ltd.	Variety	5th April 2007
121.	M/s Wolters Kluwer Health (India) Pvt. Ltd.	Current Opinion in Cardiology	5th April 2007
122.	M/s Wolters Kluwer Health (India) Pvt. Ltd.	Current Opinion in Ophthalmology	5th April 2007
123.	M/s Wolters Kluwer Health (India) Pvt. Ltd.	Current Opinion in Otolaryngology & Head and Neck Surgery	5th April 2007
124.	M/s Wolters Kluwer Health (India) Pvt. Ltd.	Obstetrics & Gynecology	5th April 2007
125.	M/s Wolters Kluwer Health (India) Pvt. Ltd.	Pancreas	5th April 2007
126.	M/s Wolters Kluwer Health (India) Pvt. Ltd.	Cornea	5th April 2007
127.	M/s Wolters Kluwer Health (India) Pvt. Ltd.	Current Opinion in Critical Care	5th April 2007
128.	M/s Wolters Kluwer Health (India) Pvt. Ltd.	Journal of Orthopaedics Trauma	5th April 2007
129.	M/s Wolters Kluwer Health (India) Pvt. Ltd.	Spine	9th April 2007

130.	M/s Wolters Kluwer Health (India) Pvt. Ltd.	American Journal of Clinical Oncology	9th April 2007
131.	M/s Wolters Kluwer Health (India) Pvt. Ltd.	Critical Care Medicine	9th April 2007
132.	M/s Wolters Kluwer Health (India) Pvt. Ltd.	Current Opinion in Endocrinology and Diabetes	9th April 2007
133.	M/s Wolters Kluwer Health (India) Pvt. Ltd.	Current Opinion in Oncology	9th April 2007
134.	M/s Wolters Kluwer Health (India) Pvt. Ltd.	Current Opinion in Pediatrics	9th April 2007
135.	M/s. Images Multimedia Private Limited	Progressive Grocer	30th April 2007
136.	M/s Reed Infomedia India Pvt. Ltd.	ICIS Chemical Business, Indian	25th May 2007
137.	M/s Springer India Pvt. Ltd.	Cardiovascular Drugs and Therapy	25th May 2007
138.	M/s Worldwide Media Pvt. Ltd.	Olive	18th July 2007
139.	M/s Wolters Kluwer (India) Pvt. Ltd.	Coronary Artery Disease	3rd August 2007
140.	M/s Wolters Kluwer (India) Pvt. Ltd.	Bone and Joint	7th August 2007
141.	M/s Wolters Kluwer (India) Pvt. Ltd.	Journal of Bronchology	7th August 2007
142.	M/s Wolters Kluwer (India) Pvt. Ltd.	Clinical Pulmonary Medicine	7th August 2007
143.	M/s Wolters Kluwer (India) Pvt. Ltd.	Otology & Neurotology	7th August 2007
144.	M/s Wolters Kluwer (India) Pvt. Ltd.	JAIDS	7th August 2007
145.	M/s Wolters Kluwer (India) Pvt. Ltd.	The Endocrinologist	7th August 2007
146.	M/s Wolters Kluwer (India) Pvt. Ltd.	Topics in Pain Management	7th August 2007

147.	M/s Wolters Kluwer (India) Pvt. Ltd.	Postgraduate Obstetrics & Gynecology	8th August 2007
148.	M/s Wolters Kluwer (India) Pvt. Ltd.	The Back Letter	8th August 2007
149.	M/s Wolters Kluwer (India) Pvt. Ltd.	Neuroreport	8th August 2007
150.	M/s Wolters Kluwer (India) Pvt. Ltd.	Current Opinion in Anesthesiology	8th August 2007
151.	M/s Wolters Kluwer (India) Pvt. Ltd.	Contemporary Critical Care	9th August 2007
152.	M/s Wolters Kluwer (India) Pvt. Ltd.	Contemporary Ophthalmology	9th August 2007
153.	M/s Wolters Kluwer (India) Pvt. Ltd.	Nutrition and the M.D.	14th August 2007
154.	M/s Wolters Kluwer (India) Pvt. Ltd.	European Journal of Emergency Medicine	14th August 2007
155.	M/s Wolters Kluwer (India) Pvt. Ltd.	ENT Today	14th August 2007
156.	M/s Wolters Kluwer (India) Pvt. Ltd.	Current Opinion in Clinical Nutrition and Metabolic Care	14th August 2007
157.	M/s Wolters Kluwer (India) Pvt. Ltd.	Menopause	14th August 2007
158.	M/s Wolters Kluwer (India) Pvt. Ltd.	The Journal of Trauma	14th August 2007
159.	M/s Wolters Kluwer (India) Pvt. Ltd.	Current Opinion in Allergy and Clinical Immunology	14th August 2007
160.	M/s Wolters Kluwer (India) Pvt. Ltd.	The Pediatric Infectious Disease Journal	14th August 2007
161.	M/s Wolters Kluwer (India) Pvt. Ltd.	Current Opinion in Infectious Disease	14th August 2007

162.	M/s Wolters Kluwer (India) Pvt. Ltd.	Current Opinion in Psychiatry	14th August 2007
163.	M/s Wolters Kluwer (India) Pvt. Ltd.	Neurology Now	14th August 2007
164.	M/s Exposure Media Marketing Pvt. Ltd.	Action Asia	23rd August 2007
165.	M/s Images Multimedia Pvt. Ltd.	GO INDIA	4th October 2007
166.	M/s Paprika Media Pvt. Ltd.	TIME OUT DELHI	22nd October 2007
167.	M/s Reed Infomedia India Pvt. Ltd.	TWICE	2nd November 2007
168.	M/s Worldwide Media Pvt. Ltd.	Good Homes	13th December 2007
169.	M/s Outlook Publishing (India) Pvt. Ltd.	People	1st January 2008
170.	M/s Outlook Publishing (India) Pvt. Ltd.	GEO	1st January 2008
171.	M/s Spenta Multimedia	HAIR	4th January 2008
172.	M/s Infomedia India Ltd.	T-3 (Tomorrow's Technology Today)	17th January 2008
173.	M/s PDA Trade Media	Airports International Indian Edition	4th April 2008
174.	M/s ITAS Media Pvt. Ltd.	Auto Bild India	11th April 2008
175.	M/s Images Multimedia Pvt. Ltd.	Sportswear International	16th April 2008
176.	M/s Reed Infomedia India Pvt. Ltd.	HOTELS	16th April 2008
177.	M/s Reed Infomedia India Pvt. Ltd.	Building Design+Construction	16th April 2008
178.	M/s Reed Infomedia India Pvt.Ltd.	Manufacturing Business Technology	16th April 2008
179.	M/s Conde Nast India Pvt. Ltd.	GQ	22nd May 2008

180.	M/s Thieme Medical and Scientific Publishers Private Ltd.	Seminars in Plastic Surgery	3rd June 2008

B. Foreign investment in Indian entities publishing scientific/ technical/speciality magazines/journals/periodicals

S.No.	NAME OF THE APPLICANT COMPANY	NAME OF MAGAZINE	DATE OF APPROVAL LETTER
1.	M/s Tata Infomedia Ltd.	Better Photography	7th April 2003
2.	M/s Tata Infomedia Ltd.	Search	3rd June 2003
3.	M/s Tata Infomedia Ltd.	Overdrive	3rd June 2003
4.	M/s Tata Infomedia Ltd.	Auto Monitor	3rd June 2003
5.	M/s Tata Infomedia Ltd.	Overdrive Grandprix	3rd June 2003
6.	M/s Tata Infomedia Ltd.	AV Max	7th May 2003
7.	M/s Tata Infomedia Ltd.	Khana Pina	20th November 2003
8.	M/s Tata Infomedia Ltd.	Yellow Line Office Guide	20th November 2003
9.	M/s Sorabjee Automotive Communications Pvt. Ltd.	Autocar India	19th February 2004
10.	M/s. Tata Infomedia Ltd.	Photo Imaging	19th February 2004
11.	M/s. Sage Publications India Ltd.	Insage	1st March 2004
12.	M/s. TBW Publishing & Media Pvt. Ltd.	Intelligent Computing Chip	1st March 2004
13.	M/s. Banyan Netfaqs Pvt. Ltd.	The Brand Reporter	1st March 2004
14.	M/s. Magz International Ltd.	Non-news and Non-current affairs publications	29th September 2004
15.	M/s. Infomedia India Ltd.	Industry Watch	27th October 2004
16.	M/s. Infomedia India Ltd.	Modern Machine Tool	27th October 2004

17.	M/s. Infomedia India Ltd.	Yellow Line City Guide	28th October 2004
18.	M/s. Quantum Information Services Ltd.	Money Simplified	11th November 2004
19.	M/s. Infomedia India Ltd.	Infomedia Yellow Pages	19th November 2004
20.	M/s. Infomedia India Ltd.	Indian Exporters Guide	19th November 2004
21.	M/s. Birla Sun Life Distribution Company Ltd.	Investime	22nd November 2004
22.	M/s. Quantum Information Services Ltd.	Equitymaster Stock Market Year Book	23rd November 2004
23.	M/s. Infomedia India Ltd.	Infomedia Home Guide	16th December 2004
24.	M/s. Infomedia India Ltd.	Infomedia City Guide	16th December 2004
25.	M/s. Haymarket SAC Publishing (India) Pvt. Ltd.	Autocar Professional	16th December 2004
26.	M/s. Indiacom Ltd.	Indiacom Yellow Pages	16th February 2005
27.	M/s. Birla Sun Life Insurance Company Ltd.	LifeLine(name changed to Birla Sun Life Lifeline)	14th March 2005 and 24th May 2005
28.	M/s. Infomedia India Ltd.	Infomedia Office Guide	14th March 2005
29.	M/s. Infomedia India Ltd.	Modern Medicare	16th March 2005
30.	M/s. Infomedia India Ltd.	Better Interiors	13th June 2005
31.	M/s. International Data Group Inc., USA	Scientific/technical magazine	16th June 2005
32.	M/s. Haymarket SAC Publishing (India) Pvt. Ltd.	WhatCar	18th July 2005
33.	M/s. Worldwide Media Ltd.	Filmfare Travel	18th July 2005

34.	M/s. IDG Media Pvt. Ltd.	Oursourcing World	24th August 2005
35.	M/s. Sage Publications India Pvt. Ltd.	Global Business Review	30th August 2005
36.	M/s. Sage Publications India Pvt. Ltd.	What HiFi	30th August 2005
37.	M/s. Worldwide Media Ltd.	The Femina Book of Good Parenting	30th August 2005
38.	M/s. Sage Publications India Pvt. Ltd.	Contribution to Indian Sociology	6th September 2005
39.	M/s. Sage Publications India Pvt. Ltd.	The Indian Economic and Social History Review	6th September 2005
40.	M/s. Sage Publications India Pvt. Ltd.	Gender Technology and Development	6th September 2005
41.	M/s. Sage Publications India Pvt. Ltd.	China Report	6th September 2005
42.	M/s. Cosmic Printmedia Pvt. Ltd.	TV Media	14th November 2005
43.	M/s. Worldwide Media Ltd.	Femina The Beauty Professional's Book	18th November 2005
44.	M/s. Saint Life Media Pvt. Ltd.	Specialist magazines/ periodicals	23rd November 2005 and 21st December 2005
45.	M/s. Infomedia India Ltd.	Cricinfo Magazine	24th February 2006
46.	M/s. Worldwide Media Ltd.	Filmfare Classics	24th February 2006
47.	M/s. Worldwide Media Ltd.	Filmfare Star Beauty	28th February 2006
48.	M/s. Worldwide Media Ltd.	Filmfare Star Homes	28th February 2006
49.	M/s. IDG Media Pvt. Ltd.	Indian Channel World	9th March 2006
50.	M/s. Worldwide Media Ltd.	Filmfare Hall of Fame	13th June 2006

51.	M/s. ICICI Prudential Life Insurance Company Ltd.	ICICI Pru Quarterly Review	6th July 2006
52.	M/s. Worldwide Media Pvt. Ltd.	Femina Homes	14th August 2006
53.	M/s Sage Publications India Pvt. Ltd.	Asian Journal of Management Cases	10th October 2006
54.	M/s Sage Publications India Pvt. Ltd.	South Asia Economic Journal	10th October 2006
55.	M/s Sage Publications India Pvt. Ltd.	Journal of Creative Communications	11th October 2006
56.	M/s Sage Publications India Pvt. Ltd.	Journal of Entrepreneurship	11th October 2006
57.	M/s Sage Publications India Pvt. Ltd.	Science, Technology & Society	11th October 2006
58.	M/s Sage Publications India Pvt. Ltd.	International Journal of Rural Management	11th October 2006
59.	M/s Sage Publications India Pvt. Ltd.	Indian Journal of Gender Studies	11th October 2006
60.	M/s Sage Publications India Pvt. Ltd.	Psychology & Developing Societies	11th October 2006
61.	M/s Sage Publications India Pvt. Ltd.	Journal of Emerging Market Finance	11th October 2006
62.	M/s Sage Publications India Pvt. Ltd.	Journal of South Asian Development	11th October 2006
63.	M/s Sage Publications India Pvt. Ltd.	Journal of Human Values	11th October 2006
64.	M/s Sage Publications India Pvt. Ltd.	Journal of Health Management	11th October 2006
65.	M/s. Sage Publications India Pvt. Ltd.	Studies in History	11th October 2006
66.	M/s Next Gen Publishing Ltd.	Permission to proceed with IPO in the Capital Market	14th November 2006
67.	M/s Infomedia India Ltd.	Disney Adventures	14th November 2006

68.	M/s Complete Wellbeing Publishing Pvt. Ltd.	Compete Wellbeing	14th November 2006
69.	M/s. Worldwide Media Ltd.	FYI	18th December 2006
70.	M/s. Worldwide Media Ltd.	Femina Allure	18th December 2006
71.	M/s. Sage Publications India Pvt. Ltd.	Journal of The School of International Studies	22nd December 2006
72.	M/s. Sage Publications India Pvt. Ltd.	Journal of Developing Societies	5th February 2007
73.	M/s. Sage Publications India Pvt. Ltd.	Progress in Development Studies	5th February 2007
74.	M/s. Sage Publications India Pvt. Ltd.	Statistical Modelling	5th February 2007
75.	M/s Thomas International Publishing Company India (P) Ltd.	TRIM Quarterly	14th February 2007
76.	M/s Worldwide Media Pvt. Ltd.	BBC Good Homes	21st February 2007
77.	M/s Haymarket SAC Publishing (India) Pvt. Ltd.	Stuff India	27th February 2007
78.	M/s Haymarket SAC Publishing (India) Pvt. Ltd.	Campaign India	3rd April 2007
79.	M/s Sage Publications India Pvt. Ltd.	South Asia Research	5th April 2007
80.	M/s Sage Publications India Pvt. Ltd.	Young – Nordic Journal of Youth Research	5th April 2007
81.	M/s Sage Publications India Pvt. Ltd.	Journal of South Asian Affairs	9th April 2007
82.	M/s. UBM India Private Limited	Computer Reseller News	27th April 2007

83.	M/s. Akar Info-media Private Limited	Construction Journal of India	30th April 2007
84.	M/s. UBM India Private Limited	Information Week	30th April 2007
85.	M/s. UBM India Private Limited	Network Computing	30th April 2007
86.	M/s Worldwide Media Pvt. Ltd.	JLT	3rd May 2007
87.	M/s Next Gen Publishing Ltd.	For Foreign Investment in the company	4th May 2007
88.	M/s Osian's – Connoisseur's of Art Private Limited	Osian's Cinemaya	15th May 2007
89.	M/s CMPMedica India Pvt. Ltd.	Orthopaedics Today	28th May 2007
90.	M/s CMPMedica India Pvt. Ltd.	Cardiology Today	28th May 2007
91.	M/s CMPMedica India Pvt. Ltd.	Paediatrics Today	28th May 2007
92.	M/s CMPMedica India Pvt. Ltd.	Ophthalmology Today	28th May 2007
93.	M/s CMPMedica India Pvt. Ltd.	Gastroenterology Today	28th May 2007
94.	M/s CMPMedica India Pvt. Ltd.	Indian Drugs Review	28th May 2007
95.	M/s CMPMedica India Pvt. Ltd.	Obs & Gynae Today	28th May 2007
96.	M/s Sage Publications India Pvt. Ltd.	The Medieval History Journal	2nd August 2007
97.	M/s Worldwide Media Pvt. Ltd.	Unplugged	14th August 2007
98.	M/s Sundaram BNP Paribas Asset Management Company Limited	The Wise Investor	14th August 2007

99.	M/s Sage Publications India Pvt. Ltd.	The Journal of Education for Sustainable Development	29th August 2007
100.	M/s Wiley India Pvt. Ltd.	For Foreign Investment for publication of speciality/technical/ scientific magazines	31st August 2007
101.	M/s CMPMedica India Private Limited	Current Index of Medical Specialities: CIMS	30th October 2007
102.	M/s Next Gen Publishing Pvt. Ltd.	The Ideal Homes and Garden	30th October 2007
103.	M/s Macmillan India Limited	Technology, Operations and Management	14th November 2007
104.	M/s IDG Media Private Limited	Windows World	14th November 2007
105.	M/s Haymarket Media (India) Private Limited	Print Week	14th November 2007
106.	M/s WAI Wire and Cable Services Pvt. Ltd.	Wire Bulletin	18th February 2008
107.	M/s Haymarket Media (India) Pvt. Ltd.	Family Physician	18th February 2008
108.	M/s Images Multimedia Pvt. Ltd.	For 26% Foreign Investment	8th April 2008
109.	M/s Infomedia India Limited	Modern Food Processing	8th April 2008
110.	M/s Infomedia India Limited	Modern Plastics and Polymers	8th April 2008
111.	M/s Infomedia India Limited	Modern Pharmaceuticals	8th April 2008
112.	M/s Infomedia India Limited	Modern Textiles	11th April 2008

113.	M/s DVV Media India Pvt. Ltd.	For 100% Foreign Investment (FDI)	15th April 2008
114.	M/s Infomedia India Limited	Modern Packaging and Design	16th April 2008
115.	M/s ITP Publishing India Pvt. Ltd.	For 100% FDI in speciality sector	24th April 2008

C. Foreign Direct Investment in Indian entities publishing newspapers and periodicals dealing in news and current affairs.

S.No.	NAME OF THE APPLICANT COMPANY	PUBLICATION	DATE OF APPROVAL LETTER
1.	M/s. HT Media Limited	News and Current Affairs publications	3rd December 2003, 7th October 2004 and 15th October 2004
2.	M/s. Business Standard Ltd.	News and Current Affairs publications	9th March 2004, 29th March 2004 and 5th April 2004
3.	M/s. Jagran Prakashan Pvt. Ltd.	News and Current Affairs publications	21st March 2005
4.	M/s. Dhara Prakashan Pvt. Ltd.	News and Current Affairs publications	6th January 2006
5.	M/s. Mid-Day Multimedia Ltd.	News and Current Affairs publications	10th January 2006
6.	M/s. The Sandesh Ltd.	News and Current Affairs publications	31st January 2006
7.	M/s. Sambhaav Media Ltd.	News and Current Affairs publications	1st February 2006
8.	M/s. Business India Publications Ltd.	News and Current Affairs publications	15th February 2006
9.	M/s Deccan Chronicle Holdings Ltd	News and Current Affairs publications	19th April 2006
10.	M/s Writers & Publishers Ltd	News and Current Affairs publications	27th April 2006
11.	M/s DT Media & Entertainment Pvt. Ltd	Education World	23rd May 2006

12.	M/s Amar Ujala Publications Limited	News and Current Affairs	30th May 2007
13.	M/s Ushodaya Enterprises Limited	News and Current Affairs (Print and Electronic Media)	27th July 2007
14.	M/s Mail Today Newspapers Private Limited	News and Current Affairs	11th October 2007
15.	M/s DB Corp Limited	News and Current Affairs	20th November 2007
16.	M/s DB Corp Limited	For allotment of shares to NRI/Visual Interactive Mauritius Limited, Mauritius	2nd May 2008
17.	HT Media Limited	For issuance of equity shares to a foreign company M/s go4i. com (Mauritius) Limited	8th May 2008

LIST OF CASES UNDER CONSIDERATION IN THE I&B MINISTRY

A. Indian edition of foreign scientific/technical/specialty magazines/ journals/ periodicals

S.No.	NAME OF THE COMPANY	NAME OF MAGAZINE	DATE OF RECEIPT OF APPLICATION & OTHER DOCUMENTS	STATUS
1.	M/s. Wolters Kluwer Health (India) Pvt. Ltd.	Retina	14th December 2006	Title not available. Company has been informed

2.	M/s. Wolters Kluwer Health (India) Pvt. Ltd.	Current Opinion in Gastroenterology	14th December 2006	-do-
3.	M/s Reed Infomedia Indian Pvt. Ltd.	B&C	30th May 2007	Title not available Company has been informed.
4.	M/s. Wolters Kluwer (India) Pvt. Ltd.	Cardiology in Review	11th June 2007	-do-
5.	M/s. Wolters Kluwer (India) Pvt. Ltd.	Continuum	11th June 2007	-do-
6.	M/s. Wolters Kluwer (India) Pvt. Ltd.	Medicine	11th June 2007	-do-
7.	M/s Reed Infomedia India Pvt. Ltd.	New Scientist	9th August 2007	-do-
8.	M/s Mediascope Publicitas (India) Pvt. Ltd.	The Banker	22nd August 2007	Final reply sent to FIPB. Title not available, company informed
9.	M/s Thieme Medical and Scientific Publishers Private Ltd.	Journal of Synthetic Organic Chemistry	10th December 2007	-do-
10.	M/s Thieme Medical and Scientific Publishers Private Ltd.	Clinics in Colon and Rectal Surgery	10th December 2007	-do-
11.	M/s publish-industry India Pvt. Ltd.	Automation & Drives (A&D)	18th December 2007	-do-

14.	M/s Media Transasia India Ltd.	Child	18th March 2008	Under Process
15.	M/s Media Transasia India Ltd.	Blender	25th March 2008	-do-
16.	M/s Strika Entertainment India Pvt. Ltd.	Supa Tiger	8th April 2008	Under Process
17.	M/s Strika Entertainment India Pvt. Ltd.	Supa Strikas	8th April 2008	Under Process
18.	M/s Outlook Publishing (India) Pvt. Ltd.	Popular Science	15th April 2008	Title not available, company has been informed
19.	M/s Media Transasia India Ltd.	CASAVIVA	23rd May 2008	Under Process
20.	M/s Next Gen Publishing Ltd.	Mother & Baby	29th May 2008	Under Process

B. Foreign investment in Indian entities publishing scientific/technical/speciality magazines/journals/periodicals

S.No.	NAME OF THE COMPANY	NAME OF MAGAZINE	DATE OF RECEIPT OF APPLICATION	STATUS
1.	M/s. Sage Publications India Pvt. Ltd.	Margin	19th February 2007	Clarification awaited from applicant company
2.	M/s. Wolters Kluwer Health (India) Pvt. Ltd.	In Focus	13th June 2007	-do-
3.	M/s. Wolters Kluwer Health (India) Pvt. Ltd.	5-Minute Consult	13th June 2007	-do-

4.	M/s. Wolters Kluwer Health (India) Pvt. Ltd.	Therapy Care Today & Tomorrow	13th June 2007	-do-
5.	M/s. Wolters Kluwer Health (India) Pvt. Ltd.	Guidelines in Practice	13th June 2007	-do-
6.	M/s. Wolters Kluwer Health (India) Pvt. Ltd.	Doctors' Voice	13th June 2007	-do-
7.	M/s. Wolters Kluwer Health (India) Pvt. Ltd.	Therapy perspective: For Rational Drug use & Disease Management	13th June 2007	-do-
8.	M/s. Indiacom Ltd.	NearBuy	7th September 2007	-do-
9.	M/s. Getit Infoservices Limited	For foreign investment	25th April, 2008	Under process

C. Foreign Direct Investment in Indian entities publishing newspapers and periodicals dealing in news and current affairs

S.No.	NAME OF THE COMPANY	NAME OF MAGAZINE	DATE OF RECEIPT OF APPLICATION	STATUS
1.	M/s. Midram Publications Pvt. Ltd.	Facsimile edition of IHT	30th November 2005	Company have been asked to clarify some points and to submit some additional documents

2.	M/s DB Corp Limited	For increase in Foreign investment as a result of investments by M/s Delight Investments Pvt. Ltd. in M/s Bhopal Financial Services Pvt. Ltd. and M/s Peacock Trading and Investment Pvt. Ltd.	26th September 2007	Company has been asked to provide clarifications, which is awaited.
3.	M/s DB Corp Limited	For increase in Foreign Investment by way of issuing IPO	19th December 2007	Under process
4.	M/s Lokmat Newspapers Private Limited	For FDI by M/s Dunearn Investments (Mauritius) Pvt. Ltd and M/s Park Equity Holding Limited.	9th May 2008	Company has been asked to provide clarifications, which is awaited.
5.	M/s Prithvi Prakashan Private Limited	-do-	-do-	-do-

Appendix III

Broadcasting Services Regulation Bill-2007 on Cross Media Ownership

Restrictions on accumulation of interest:

(1) *The Central Government shall have the authority to prescribe such eligibility conditions and restrictions with regard to accumulation of interest at national, state or local level in the broadcast segments of the media by the print or other media as may be considered necessary from time to time, to prevent monopolies across different segments of the media as well as within the broadcast segments, to ensure plurality and diversity of news and views.*

(2) *No content broadcasting service provider together with its interconnected undertakings shall have more than the prescribed share of paid up equity or have any other financing or commercial arrangement that may give it management control over the financial, management or editorial policies of any broadcasting network service provider.*

> *Provided that this condition will not be applicable in cases where a content broadcasting service provider requires a teleport or such other infrastructure for captive use to make its content available to other broadcasting network service providers.*

(3) *No broadcasting network service provider together with its interconnected undertakings shall have more than the prescribed share of paid up equity or have any other financing or commercial arrangement that may give it management control over the financial, management or editorial policies of any content broadcasting service provider.*

(4) *No content broadcasting service provider together with its interconnected undertakings shall have more than the prescribed share of the total number of channels in a city or a state subject to a prescribed overall ceiling for the whole country.*

(5) *The restrictions as required under subsections (1) to (4) above shall be laid down by the Central Government in consultation with the Authority, on the basis of a review to be conducted every 3 years by the Authority.*

Provided that till such a review is done by the Authority and restrictions revised by the Government the prescribed share under subsection(2) and (3) shall be taken as 20% and the overall ceiling on the total number of channels under subsection(4) as 15%. Provided further that in a subsequent review the Central Government shall not reduce the prescribed share to a level below that prescribed under first proviso.

Provided further that any broadcasting service provider, in breach of the restrictions as provided under the first proviso of this subsection, shall submit his compliance plan to the Government within two months and shall come into compliance within one year of the coming into force of this Act.